# Super Staff

# SuperVision

### A How-To Handbook of Powerful Techniques To Lead Camp Staff to Be Their Best

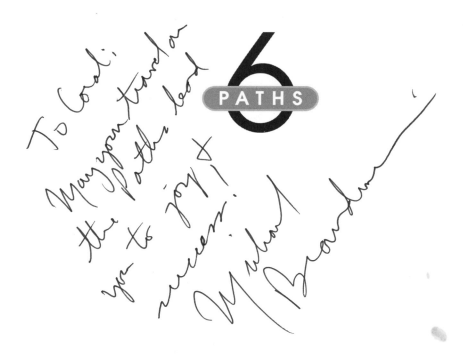

**6 PATHS**

*To Coral:
May your travels on
the Paths lead
you to joy &
success!
Michael Brandwein*

# MICHAEL BRANDWEIN

# Super Staff SuperVision

## A How-To Handbook of Powerful Techniques to Lead Camp Staff to Be Their Best

For inquiries, please contact the author at:
Michael Brandwein
5 Coventry Lane
Lincolnshire, IL 60069
(847) 940-9820
michaelbrandwein.com

ISBN 0-9670321-1-3

Library of Congress Control Number: 2001127027

Printed in the United States of America

# The Pages In Front
# That People Don't Read

This is my second book, unless you count the three legal thrillers I ghost-wrote last summer for a *New York Times* best-selling author, whose name I cannot disclose due to contractual restrictions.

My first book was about training staff. This book focuses on supervising staff. We'll be working a lot in this book on the central core of supervision, which is support. So it's fitting to take a moment now to thank the people who have supported me in this project.

My wife Donna and I have two wonderful boys, David and Benjamin. David, currently in seventh grade, took one look at the title of this book, thought for a maximum of five seconds, and said, "Triple S, V, that's the way we should be." Thirteen years old, and he's already making up acronyms. He is definitely my son. I love you, David.

Benjamin, currently in third grade, asked me months ago if he would be mentioned in the dedication of the book. I said that of course he would. But a few weeks ago, when Ben was looking through hundreds of pages of drafts, he said sadly, "I don't see a dedication part." I told him I hadn't written it yet. He looked sad again, so I asked him what was wrong. He said, "I wanted to be dedicated earlier." I love you, Ben.

Speaking of dedication: You are only holding this book in your hand because my office manager made it possible. Her editing and production work were—well, I checked my thesaurus for something powerful enough to replace "extraordinary" and "stellar" and the only words it listed were "Sara Wolfersberger." Thank you Sara—my respect and appreciation for you is boundless. I mean, *are* boundless....

A special thank you for the support of two dear friends and brilliant professionals, John Powers and Bruce Muchnick. Writing can be lonely work, and John and Bruce held the brightest of flashlights for me at the end of some intimidating tunnels. Thanks also to Tom Greensfelder, our cover designer, for his creativity and expertise, and Lee Levin, master of many talents, for his photography and friendship.

To my readers, thank you for the hard work you do to help our children become their best. I hope this book helps you in your efforts. I know the book is not perfect, and I know it is not complete. There are so many important supervision issues that I could not fit into one manageable volume. I hope that you will look forward to exploring these with me in a later book.

I dedicate this book to Jack and Helen Pearse, Jane McCutcheon, and John Jorgenson, directors of Camp Tawingo in Huntsville, Ontario, and Larry and Pearl Bell, directors of Camp Robin Hood, in Markham, Ontario. Your mentorship, support, and friendship have meant more to me than I can adequately express here. I have so admired the differences you continue to make in the world, and your guidance and graciousness have made it possible for me to follow in your Paths. I will be forever grateful.

Finally, I also dedicate this book to Donna, but more importantly, I dedicate my life and my love to her as well. She is and will always be my best friend. Nothing important is possible without her; nothing is impossible with her. Donna, thanks for walking the most important Paths of life with your hand in mine. I love you.

# Where To Find Stuff

1  You Want Me to Supervise *Adults*? . . . . . . . . . . . . . . . . . .2
2  The Importance of Effective Camp Supervision . . . . . . .6
3  The Role Truth About Supervision  . . . . . . . . . . . . . . . .7
4  SuperVision: Paths to Success . . . . . . . . . . . . . . . . . . . . .9
5  **Path 1 / Add Creative Twists to Program** . . . . . . . . .14
6  **Path 2 / Praise Positive Staff Behavior** . . . . . . . . . .33
7  An Excellent Boss Always Knows the SOSS . . . . . . . .45
8  Praise in Creative Ways . . . . . . . . . . . . . . . . . . . . . . . .53
9  **Path 3 / Support Staff & Help Them Grow** . . . . . . .57
10 Highering Staff to Motivate Success . . . . . . . . . . . . . .62
11 Supporting Staff Who Are Dealing with
      Challenging Children . . . . . . . . . . . . . . . . . . . . . . . . .78
12 Reverse Engineering  . . . . . . . . . . . . . . . . . . . . . . . . . .95
13 **Path 4 / Manage Undesired Staff Behavior in
      Positive Ways** . . . . . . . . . . . . . . . . . . . . . . . . . . . . .100
14 Using Questions to Teach Problem-Solving &
      Decision-Making . . . . . . . . . . . . . . . . . . . . . . . . . . .111
15 Smoothies . . . . . . . . . . . . . . . . . . . . . . . . . . . . . . . . .121
16 Tools for Tact . . . . . . . . . . . . . . . . . . . . . . . . . . . . . .122
17 **Path 5 / Help Campers Who Need
      Extra Support**  . . . . . . . . . . . . . . . . . . . . . . . . . . . .127
18 Danny: The Power of Path 5 . . . . . . . . . . . . . . . . . . .135
19 **Path 6 / Keep Camp Safe**  . . . . . . . . . . . . . . . . . . .140
20 Pathways Meetings: 10 Tips  . . . . . . . . . . . . . . . . . . .147
21 Leading Effective Staff Meetings  . . . . . . . . . . . . . . . .152
22 Modeling & The Pass Down Principle . . . . . . . . . . . .159
23 Super Tips for SuperVision Success  . . . . . . . . . . . . . .163
24 We Will Path This Way Again... . . . . . . . . . . . . . . . . .167

*The Liver*
A  SOSS: Xcellent Xamples . . . . . . . . . . . . . . . . . . . . . .169
B  Reverse Engineering: Sample Skill List . . . . . . . . . . . .187
C  Questions That Help Teach
      Problem-Solving to Staff . . . . . . . . . . . . . . . . . . . . . .196

# Chapter One

# You Want Me to Supervise Adults?

My path to becoming a staff supervisor was, I think, a typical one. I had successfully fooled people into believing that I was good at working with children as a group counselor and specialist. Then the call came at the end of a summer, offering me a promotion to the position of a staff supervisor. I was very flattered, accepted, hung up the phone, and wondered when I'd get caught.

I didn't know anything about supervising *adults*. What I knew about was kids. Somebody was going to catch on. They were going to figure out that I was monumentally unqualified. Worse, I was too young. Some of the people I'd be supervising had been working at camps a lot longer than I had. Double worse, a few of them were school teachers, who, apparently seized by some psychotic impulse, were spending their summers working with children at camp. I was going to be their *boss*? What's wrong with this picture?

## The First Meeting

It's a few days before orientation begins and I show up for my first meeting as a supervisor. I haven't done anything to prepare for my new role as a supervisor. I don't know how to. I have no one to ask. I'm sitting with the assistant director and two other supervisors, both of whom are school teachers—one high school, and the other pre-school. Very nice. Older.

Everyone else in the room has new clipboards. They look solid and shiny. They look like the sort of clipboard that a supervisor should be carrying around. I've brought my battered counselor's clip board from last summer.

So I'm sitting in this meeting. This is the part I remember best. The assistant director is telling us a bunch of stuff that we need to do to get camp ready, and I'm writing almost none of it down.

This is embarrassing for me to admit to you, but the reason for my lack of writing was that I was desperately trying to look qualified for my new position. I thought, immaturely and erroneously, that if I took notes it might look like I didn't know this stuff already. So I didn't take many notes.

## If Only....

Considering my feelings of insecurity, I look back on that meeting and wonder why I didn't just say something like, "Would you be willing to tell us some of the things you expect from us as supervisors?" Why didn't I take the assistant director or one of the other supervisors aside and say, "You've been a supervisor before. This is my first time. I'd really appreciate it if you could give me some idea of what to expect." And why didn't I ask these questions?:

"What are some things that you know now that you wish someone had told you when you first started?"

"What do you think are the most important things for a supervisor to do? How do you do them?"

"How do you build a good, positive relationship with staff so that you don't walk around all day looking like you're trying to catch them doing something wrong?"

"What if they mess up—what do you say?"

"How do you do this job and stay creative and play with the kids, which is why we got into this in the first place?"

"What have been the hardest challenges for you, and what are some good ways to handle these?"

"Where did you get that cool clipboard?"

I wasn't smart enough to ask. But please note: nobody offered to tell me, either.

During orientation, staff received training on how to work with children. But as a supervisor, I didn't get any training on how to work with staff. Zero.

It became immediately clear that my training had to be "on the job" after the staff and campers had arrived, and I was basically left to conduct that training myself. I watched what the other supervisors did, and fortunately, because they were good, I learned some positive things. I learned mostly, though, through my mistakes. I worked hard and did my best.

I look back on that first time as a camp administrator and wonder how much more effective I could have been if I had been able to study and think about *how* to supervise before I did it.

## Tools for Training

The time to train supervisors is often very limited. And it's a hard enough job for directors and assistant directors to put together the curriculum for staff training, let alone have an extra 30 seconds to put one together for the training of supervisors.

So that's why I've written this book. The questions that I should have asked are answered here. The things that I wish people had told me before I started are described in these pages. Opportunities to practice supervision skills are here as well.

Being a camp staff supervisor is a very challenging job. But it's also an exhilarating kick, and when we do our work well, we can make positive and lasting differences in the lives of both children and staff. I hope that this book gives you lots of tools to help you do that work.

## Big Bonus in the Liver

I mentioned in *Training Terrific Staff* that it didn't make much sense to put important, useful stuff in a back section of a book called the "Appendix," because that is something that can cause great pain and that you really can do without. So I called the section at the end of that book the "Liver" and will continue that tradition here.

The Liver contains three sections, containing hundreds of specific examples of skills and techniques.

## Pencil Point

You will see this symbol in several parts of this book:

These are times for you to practice a bit by doing some thinking and writing on your own before reading further.

You will also see this symbol:

These are times for you to floss thoroughly.

## Using This Book

If you are a camp director, you can use this book to train and lead staff supervisors. You will also be able to use these techniques when you deal directly with staff. Please have your supervisors read this book. Talk to them about the points that you feel are most important to success at your camp. Speak to them about how you want to use the Paths approach and set up the Pathways meetings that are described here. Invite them to ask questions, and encourage them to use the book as a resource as they walk the Paths and meet challenges throughout the summer.

If you are a new staff supervisor, welcome, and congratulations. This book was written to help you make this transition with confidence and skill. And don't worry—every single thing you have used to lead children will work very well in leading staff— who are just older children.

Finally, if you have supervised before, welcome back. This book will build on your experience and give you lots of new things to try that will keep you motivated and recharged to make this the very best season yet.

## Chapter Two

# The Importance of Effective Camp Supervision

This is the introductory chapter of the book where I am supposed to take about seven to eight pages to explain the *importance* of effective camp supervision. Here I discuss the effect of supervisors on the performance of staff. I mention that selecting excellent staff and providing them with superb training are the cornerstones of camp success. I then illustrate, using numerous examples, that much of a staff person's leadership development takes place "on the job" and that such development can only be assured by skilled supervisors.

But what I *really* want to talk to you about is not philosophy, but the specific things you and I can do and say every day to make an immediate, positive difference for staff and campers.

So here's the deal. I say, let's just declare all of this "importance" talk a huge "duh," skip it, and get to the good stuff.

See you in Chapter Three. Race you.....

## Chapter Three

# The Role Truth
# About Supervision

The single most important word that describes a supervisor's role is *support*. Once we understand this, we're heading straight for success.

By "support," we mean supporting the staff. A supervisor's most important task is to walk around asking a single question: *"What can I do to help staff do their very best work?"*

Our job is to support staff because it's staff who most directly provide the service of camp—giving children enriching experiences that last a lifetime. Unfortunately, organizational charts don't always make this concept clear because "staff" get put at the bottom, with the "bosses" on top. Actually, the bosses are the foundation, or the floor, on which the staff can stand to directly serve the children.

You know the word association tests, where we're given a word and asked to say the first word that comes to mind? They say ice cream, we might say cone. They say shoe, we might say foot.

I have found that when such words are presented to managers, if we give them the word "supervisor," a large number of them don't reply with the word "support" as a first response. And even if supervisors do believe that "support" is their central responsibility, what really matters is the answer to *this* question: "Do all of the people we are supervising *know* that we believe this?" I have learned from workshop discussions that many *employees* do not first think of "support" when they hear the words "supervisor" or "boss."

## Two Tasks

So we have two tasks. First we must understand that our primary role as a supervisor is to provide support to others. Second, we must act in ways that credibly communicate to staff that we actually believe that this is our primary role. Otherwise, when staff hear the words "boss" or "supervisor" they may first think "look out!" or "heads up" or "watch your back!"

Perhaps some negative perceptions of "supervisor" exist because it is not a very warm word. I use the term in this book because it's a very common way to describe a variety of camp administrative positions. But when it comes to giving supervisors an actual job title, words like "team leader" may convey a more positive relationship.

## Providing the Support

So how do we provide this support to staff? We can do it by walking six Paths. These Paths make up what I call the SuperVision system, and I'll provide an overview of this system in the next chapter.

# Chapter Four

# SuperVision:
# Paths to Success

## The SuperVision System

We can make dramatic improvements in camp staff supervision, and we can do it right away. The SuperVision system has two key elements:

1. **Responsibility**: We need to be more clear about what we expect supervisors to do when they are walking around camp.

2. **Accountability & Communication**: We need to set up a simple method to make sure that these things get done.

## Effective Supervision Requires Vision

We could make camp supervision much more exciting and fulfilling if we had a crisp *vision* of all of the ways in which we can make a positive difference in camp every day.

In my early days as a camp supervisor, I found myself mostly walking around reacting to problems, questions, and concerns. Of course I smiled and waved to groups of kids and said hello to staff. I'd jump into a game or join an activity whenever I could. I remember smiling and saying "Howzitgoin?"a lot, which for about a week represented the full extent of my supervisor vocabulary.

Here's what I was missing. I was spending the majority of my time "weeding and pruning the camp garden." If I saw something that wasn't supposed to be there, I weeded it out. If one bush was getting in the way of another, I pruned away the conflict to make sure everything remained in its proper place.

What I *wasn't* doing was walking around promoting *growth*. I mean, of course the weeding and pruning helped things grow that were already planted, but I wasn't putting new or better plants into the ground. I wasn't looking for great ways to upgrade the overall garden.

A lot of supervisor burnout comes from constantly dealing with problems and other difficult issues. If you ask most camp supervisors for their daily goals, they'll say things like "help the staff" and "make sure everything is going smoothly" and "deal with any problems that come up." *Supervisor motivation, like staff motivation, greatly increases when there are specific, positive, and challenging goals to reach.*

## Responsibility: The Paths Approach

As we walk around camp using the Paths approach, we will be doing six jobs to help staff and campers be their best. Yes, we'll also pass messages to people from time to time and handle some administrative details. But our main purpose will be to work on these six specific responsibilities.

I call each responsibility a Path. These are the six Paths:

**Path 1:  Add creative twists to program**

☐  to make camp more exciting and boost participation and motivation

**Path 2:  Praise positive staff behavior**

☐  to reinforce and grow more of the skills and
choices that we most value

**Path 3:  Support staff and help them grow**

☐  so they do their best work and are motivated by
reaching personal goals

**Path 4:  Manage undesired staff behavior in
positive ways**

☐  to get staff to replace bad choices with good ones
and learn how to develop better independent
decision-making and problem-solving

**Path 5:  Help campers who need extra support**

☐  because they are unconnected to others, are not
enjoying the full camp experience, or have other
special concerns

**Path 6:  Keep camp safe**

☐  not only physically (outside safety) but
emotionally (inside safety)

Each of these Paths will be described in its own chapter. Most of
the Paths are then followed by supporting chapters that provide
additional techniques for SuperVision success.

## Adapt the Paths to Your Needs

Please do not feel limited by the number of Paths I've selected.
After you've read about the Paths, you can adapt this approach to
best fit the needs of your particular camp. For example, you might
want to eliminate some Paths or add some—although staying with
a manageable number is important. You might find it helpful to
consolidate two Paths into one or describe them differently. Our

goal is to just make sure that we have specific areas of exciting and challenging responsibilities that supervisors can work on every day.

## Accountability & Communication: The Pathways Meeting

Supervisors ordinarily have conversations with their boss (camp director, assistant director, or other senior camp administrator—I'll use the word director here to include all of these) many times during a camp week. Our SuperVision system adds a specially scheduled weekly conversation which we call the Pathways meeting.

Each supervisor sets up a regular time for this meeting with the director. It's the same time each week. While the nature of camp will sometimes require that these meetings be rescheduled, the key is to set aside a special priority time for them and try our best to work other things around them. If circumstances in a particular week require that the time or day of the meeting be changed, that's OK—but we just have to be sure that the meeting takes place once per week.

How long should the meeting be? At least 15 or 20 minutes should be blocked out, and then if further discussion is desired or necessary, it can continue or be set for a later time.

What happens at the meeting? We'll provide more details in Chapter 20, but basically the supervisor and director talk about specific things the supervisor has done during the past week on each of the six Paths. The supervisor can also use the director as a resource during these meetings to help plan and support future work on the Paths.

## Four Big Benefits from the Pathways Meetings

There are four benefits provided by these weekly Pathways meetings:

1.  What makes the SuperVision system work is that *every supervisor knows that once a week they will be expected to speak in these special meetings about what they have done in six specific Paths of responsibilities.* This provides a big motivation to supervisors to make sure that they are working regularly in each of these areas.

2.  These meetings are *terrific opportunities for supervisors to ask questions* and benefit from the directors' expertise.

3.  The Pathways meetings provide a *specific and regularly scheduled way for supervisors to get feedback and recognition for their work.* Supervising can be very lonely and this is a chief cause of supervisor burnout. It is very important for directors to get information on a regular basis about how supervisors are using their time and skills. These meetings also provide supervisors a chance to share their successes.

4.  *The meetings help directors evaluate the performance of supervisors.* Evaluating the work of supervisors can be hard. If the part of camp for which a supervisor is responsible is going well and doesn't have any major problems, then we tend to believe that the supervisor is doing a good job. But if we really probed more deeply, we'd ask, "To what extent is this success due to specific things done by the supervisor? What exactly has the supervisor contributed to make things go so well?"

    The Pathways meetings provide specific answers to these two questions because supervisors will have a regular opportunity to talk about their contributions and provide examples of what they have done.

## Paths to Success

There were many times as a supervisor when I wasn't sure about what I was supposed to be doing or how I could best be spending my time. The SuperVision system solves that problem in a positive way by providing specific and valuable things to work on with staff and campers and regular opportunities to discuss this work with experienced professionals.

It's time now to describe the Paths in greater detail and identify specific techniques that will help make our travels on these Paths a great success.

## Chapter Five

# Add Creative Twists To Program

Out of the six Paths, this one is definitely the most fun. It's a reason to jump out of bed in the morning feeling jazzed—because that's exactly what we're going to do to camp. We're going to wake people up. We're going to take them by surprise. We're going to electrify everyone with fresh ideas that will keep them guessing every day about what cool, crazy, challenging, fun, unpredictable thing will happen next.

Supervisors have to deal with difficult behavior and challenging problems. As we focus on these things day after day, it's normal to feel that we've gotten away from the joy that brought us to camp in the first place. We may feel that we've lost touch with the satisfaction of just "playing with the kids." I bet there hasn't been a camp supervisor in history who hasn't from time to time wished to be back serving as a group counselor or an instructor.

So please stay tuned in. In this chapter, we'll see how Path 1 is the cure for these blues. On Path 1, we don't just get to play with the kids in one camp group. We get to play with the *whole camp*. And the looks on the faces of kids—and staff, too—as we show them great new stuff will be one of the biggest payoffs we get as we walk the Paths every day.

## Our Goal

Our goal is simple. We want camp to stay interesting. *Not only to our campers, but to our staff.* We want to maximize attention, interest, motivation, and participation.

At camp, our enemy is boredom. We don't like people "sitting out." We don't like it when campers declare that something is "boring" or that they don't want to do it.

It's important to understand that the main cause of boredom is predictability. When campers first participate in activities, these are new experiences and interest is high. But once the newness wears off, campers may become less involved. They feel less challenged. As they become less interested in participating, they may engage in distracting or other undesired behavior.

So if campers are doing soccer or archery or climbing every week, our mission is to try to ensure that when they do these activities the fifth time, it's not exactly the same way they did them the prior four times. There should be something new and fresh every time campers engage in the activity.

## Our Responsibility

Our best staff ask themselves every day how they can keep things interesting for campers. That's one of the things that makes these leaders best. But many staff will need our support to show them the wide variety of choices they can make to maximize the fun and participation every day.

*Supervisors are a portable resource for staff.* It's an important part of our daily job to introduce new ideas or variations to activities and program and to teach staff to do this themselves.

## Attention, Please!

Attention comes from *contrast*. Whenever expectations are violated, attention goes up. An important secret is that the change does not have to be a big one. Even small, easy changes to an activity can cause big boosts in attention and participation.

15

So every time we lead children, we want to ask this important question: "*What can we do that will take our campers by surprise?*"

## What Place Does Creativity Have at Camp?

I've had people say to me, "But the kids love to look forward to certain things, and if we change how we do them, they'll be disappointed." Introducing twists and new program ideas does not mean throwing out tradition or abandoning what works.

Suppose that "Gold Rush" is our campers' favorite special event. This program goes so far back in camp history that it predates the actual historical event....

So we're not going to get rid of Gold Rush. What we're going to do is to challenge ourselves and our staff to continue to find new ways to make it engaging and interesting. Applying creativity doesn't mean that the Old Prospector isn't going to show up at camp this summer. But it means that we *can* find a new way for him to enter, or a new reason for him to be here, or a new crisis or challenge that campers need to respond to in order to help him.

Traditions bring campers back year after year, but so does keeping camp fresh with new challenges and opportunities.

Finally, it is important that we develop creativity in our children. And we must prepare them to deal confidently with change. So we, as the adults at camp, must be a model for our campers of how to be creative and open to new ideas.

## Let's Do the Twist

I use a simple two-question technique to help bring freshness to camp. Pick a camp program or activity or regular routine that you want to make more interesting and then ask these two camp creativity questions:

### One: What do campers expect?

This means asking:

- ☐ What do campers expect when they come to this activity or participate in this routine?
- ☐ What are the usual procedures?
- ☐ How are things usually done?
- ☐ What do campers usually see, hear, and do?

16

- ☐   What do staff usually do or say?
- ☐   Where does it take place?
- ☐   What equipment is used?

## Two: How can we mess it up?

This means asking:

- ☐   What could we change that would be unexpected by campers? Again, this doesn't have to be a complete overhaul or a huge thing—just something to create contrast.
- ☐   What would be something we could do differently that wouldn't interfere with the goals of the activity and would take campers by surprise?

Answering questions one and two is actually a lot of fun. When I present these questions in training at a camp, I first ask staff to try answering them on their own for about two minutes. Then I get them into small groups of three or four to exchange their ideas and brainstorm about more.

*We should do this during training*

For example: this past summer when I asked one camp staff to think about the two creativity questions, specialists got together in their different areas to brainstorm. After a few moments the gymnastics folks came up with several simple ideas. Somersaults were great warm-ups, they said, but they got boring very quickly. So first, they would spice up regular somersaults with hoops held on the ground that campers could tumble through.

Second, they would put masking tape in the shape of numbers or letters on the mats, and just before a tumbler began they would call out the number or letter that the camper had to hit on the somersault. Third, when campers entered the gymnastics area, they usually sat in a circle to do warm-up exercises. The instructors decided that every day they would have campers sit in a different formation: squares, triangles, rectangles, and other shapes. They would explain, they decided, that the different shapes were a reminder for campers to stay in "shape" and that one of the benefits of gymnastics is to help them do so. This is only a little change, but it's something that helps make the activity fresh. Adding even a little spice to the beginning helps motivate campers to start with a positive attitude.

When I do the two-question creativity activity with staff, the immediate flood of terrific ideas is remarkable. What most impresses me is the speed with which staff can do this. In just five or six minutes, they come up with dozens of really exciting twists that get the whole room totally energized. Staff really get motivated, often saying that they can't wait to try their ideas.

## Practice One: Getting a Bigger Kick Out of Soccer

I'd like you to try asking the two camp creativity questions yourself. Suppose that we want to make soccer fresh. It's not that the children don't like soccer. Actually, most of them do. But we want our camp to be a place where we do the extraordinary. Kids can play regular soccer at home. At camp, we make it special.

So please ask yourself:

1. What does soccer usually look like (what do they expect)?
2. What are some possible things we could change?

Please grab some paper and write your ideas. Just let your brain go wild for about three minutes. But before you begin...

## A Special Note, or, The Author Acts Like Your Mom for a Moment

Some readers might be tempted to just skip this activity and go straight to the examples. Not you, of course, but some other people.

I do hope that the examples I will provide here and elsewhere in other chapters will be some of the most valuable parts of this entire book. But if you read the examples before you try writing down your own ideas first, you'll blow an opportunity to hone your skills. It's kind of like reading the answers to a puzzle before you try doing it yourself. That approach won't help you get any better at doing puzzles.

So please don't read ahead yet– take a few minutes now and see what you can come up with. Thanks!

So how did you do? I'm betting that you came up with lots of easy ways to jazz up soccer. Here is a list of some of the potential twists that we could make to soccer to create contrast and take our campers by surprise. Please pay particular attention to the very first one. It's my favorite, it's easy, and it should be in the repertoire of every camp supervisor:

## Some Creative Variations for Soccer

☐ play with more than one ball at a time (and change the number as you go: begin with two, then three, then still more)

☐ use a different type of ball, like a beach ball, a tennis ball, or a ping-pong ball

☐ don't even use a ball; substitute another object (an old pillow, a towel rolled up with rubber-bands, a sock)

☐ increase the number of goals (for example, put four more on the sidelines, or two right next to each other at each end of the field)

☐ change the location of the goals (put one or more in the middle of the field, marked by cones, and perhaps attackable from all sides)

☐ make the field smaller

☐ change the shape of the field

☐ change the size of the goals

☐ have more goalies in each goal

☐ have no goalies

☐ give the goalies a bucket of water balloons and let them score points for their team if they hit anyone

☐ put targets in the goal, like wiffle balls on top of safety cones; hit them for extra points (this can be done with a goalie or with no goalie); make different targets worth different amounts of points

☐ use safety cones or other soft objects like towels or shirts to mark out "danger zones" on the field; if a player steps into the zone or kicks the ball through one, it's a point for the other team (it's cool to let teams place their own zones so they can figure out strategic locations for each; each zone can be made with no more than, for example, eight towels or shirts)

☐ when you shout "flip," the teams have to immediately switch goals and their direction of play

☐ when you shout "link," the players must link arms with another player and move together in pairs; when you shout "triple link" they move as triplets; if the team doesn't divide up evenly into two's or three's, the extra players can be assigned to the goal

☐ no player can pass unless they've kicked the ball (short dribbles) three times first

☐ players tie a piece of crepe paper around their non-dominant leg and must contact the ball only with that leg; use of the wrong leg causes loss of possession, or a point for the other side

Would we play an entire soccer game using one or more of these variations? We could. The "danger zone" idea—especially if zones are changed throughout a game—is just one of the twists that will sustain interest for an entire period. But mostly, the ideas that we've come up with are opportunities to add some spice and flavor to a regular activity period. It's fun to break up a regular game to play for a few moments using special rules or other changes.

*One of the most important times to use these twists is during warm-ups.* Most campers and staff are not particularly fond of the unfortunately named "drills." Sounds as inviting as oral surgery, doesn't it? Pre-game practice doesn't have to be boring. Any one of the ideas on our list of soccer variations will grab attention and teach some terrific skills at the same time.

Plus—and this is very important—the way we begin an activity sets the tone for the entire period. If we begin with a strong first impression, it's easier to keep enthusiasm high.

## Practice Two: Making Baseball a Bigger Hit

What things could we change in baseball? Try it now, please, before you look at the ideas that follow.

How did you do? Here are some ideas:

☐ change the order in which they run the bases (start by running to third base)

☐ change the number and location of the bases

☐ change the distance separating the bases

☐ change where the batter stands (how about in center field or at first base?)

☐ change the bat to a broom or field hockey stick

☐ change the shape, size, or type of ball (does it even have to be a ball?)

☐ give small boxes (no sharp edges) or big paper bags with handles to fielders to be used to catch the ball (we can try two fielders holding one paper bag, and increase the number of fielders)

☐ tape a water balloon or balloons to the bat; points can be given for breaking a balloon, or points can be deducted for breaking one

☐ tape water balloons on the bases or place them on the field or in the base lines; anyone who breaks one loses a point for their team

☐ my all-time favorite: when the batter gets a hit, the batter's entire team runs to first base (you should see the look on the first baseman's face when the entire group comes running down the base line!); they all have to hold hands (only one camper needs to be touching first base; only one camper needs to be tagged out to get the whole group); they move around the bases in this manner; whoever bats next breaks out of the group and runs to the batter's box

21

At a day camp where I did some mid-summer training, a supervisor proudly walked me over to a baseball field and showed me one of the most terrific examples of a creative program twist that I've ever seen. The campers were playing kickball. But then there were gymnastics mats set up which stretched from home plate to first base. When the batter kicked the ball, she or he had to somersault to first base. Then there were mats set up to create a tunnel from first base to second. There was a springboard to jump on and some hoops to crawl through to get from second to third. And from third base to home was a limbo thing followed by a maze of hoops that they had to step in and out of (like football players stomping through auto tires).

The kids and staff were having a blast—but what was this activity, kickball or gymnastics? I asked the supervisor and she just smiled and said, "Guess." That's what was so great about what the supervisor and staff had done. Because of the interweaving of different skills and equipment from so many different areas, there was no way to be sure which scheduled activity this was. The supervisor had worked with the staff to inject creative fun while teaching lots of terrific skills.

## Practice Three: Better Beds

Yes, at resident camps, the one activity that is at the top of most campers' list of heart-pounders is making their beds in the morning. But suppose you decided to push the cardiac envelope and really liven it up even more. Please do some writing now on your own before you continue reading. What might you change to take campers by surprise?

Here are some ideas:

- ☐ make the bed using only one hand (to make it extra hard: the non-dominant hand)

- ☐ two people make a bed together, but one can use only their left hand and the other can use only their right

- ☐ everyone puts a large sock over each of her or his shoes (for cleanliness); the covered shoes are then placed on their hands; now they make the bed, alone or with partners

- ☐ play music; when it stops, everyone freezes; if they get caught, they must start over (or don't have any "penalty" at all—just keep on playing)

- ☐ some campers make their beds with something in them that will stick up under the covers; other campers have to guess what the hidden object is (try allowing yes/no questions as another variation)

- ☐ everyone makes their own bed until the leader shouts "rotate"—at which point each camper moves to the bed on the right (or below, if an upper bunk bed) and continues making that one until the next "rotate;" on "reverse rotate" everyone goes back to the left (or up); this can be done using musical cues for the rotations (when the music gets louder they go to the right; softer, they go to the left)

- ☐ they take the mattress outside, "make it," and then bring it back inside

## Practice Four: A Swinging Test at the Playground

When I was a young counselor, we'd sometimes have "free choice" on the schedule when our group could go to whatever area we wanted. Often, the area we'd choose would be already taken. So I would sometimes pick areas that nobody cared about and try to make them riveting. I'd say, "Let's go to the playground." My guys would roll their eyes, of course, and say, "Playground?! Are you kidding? That's for little kids...."

> I'd stand very, very still, arch one eyebrow (yes, I admit it—I've practiced this in the mirror; are you going to deny doing the same?) and say very, very quietly: "Oh, really?" We walked over to the playground, and once my campers saw the cool stuff we could do there, the playground became one of our favorite places. Please note that I said "our." That's a key point to understand about creative twists. They are great for the campers, but also great for the staff.

Our job on Path 1 means walking around every day looking for new ways to use old things. One of my favorite things to ask when visiting a camp is whether they have a playground. Most day camps do, and some resident camps may have them if they serve younger campers. If the playground exists, it's the first place I go when I want to practice Path 1 with supervisors.

Here's what I say to the supervisors at the playground. "This is an area that's intended for younger kids. So here's the challenge. We've got five minutes. Our mission is to think about the expected use for each piece of equipment and fire off as many ways as possible to change or use it so that older campers would want to play here, too. Of course our ideas can be used by younger campers, but if we do this right, the older ones will actually want to pick this area for their free choice activity and will try to drive the little kids away."

Please try this yourself now. Make a list of basic playground equipment (slide, swings, jungle gyms, monkey bars, etc.) and write down how you would use these items in unexpected ways.

Here are some of my favorite ideas with several pieces of playground equipment:

## The Slide

- ☐ we can use it to roll or shove objects of different sizes and weights (marbles, ping-pong balls, tennis balls, volley balls, coins, bean bags, flying discs on edge, and so on)

- ☐ we can put a bucket, box or other container at the end to catch these things

- ☐ one camper at the top of the slide rolls a ball down while one or more campers at the bottom throw other objects at the rolled ball; if they hit it on its way down, they get a point; if the ball makes it all the way to the bottom without being hit, the roller gets a point

- ☐ campers can make their own pinball machine by duct-taping things to the slide (small balloons, toilet paper tubes, etc.) to create bumpers that change the paths of the rolled objects

- ☐ numbered paper targets can be taped to the slide at various heights and positions, to be hit by a ball, bean bag, flying disc, or other object

- ☐ squares, circles, triangles, and other shapes can be made with pieces of tape on the slide; when the name of a shape is called out, campers have to hit that shape with a bouncy ball; as an additional challenge, we can also have them try to catch the ball on the rebound

- ☐ the ladder on the slide can be used in many creative ways; please see Jungle Gyms, below....

## Jungle Gyms (Squares, Domes, or Other Structures to Climb On)

- ☐ the criss-crossed grids that make up this piece of equipment are just shouting to be made into target holes for balls, bean bags, flying discs, rolled socks (I call the socks version "laundry machine"), and so on

- we can tape numbers on particular openings to indicate the number of points awarded for throwing objects through those openings

- we can tape letters of the alphabet to openings and challenge campers to throw through the correct openings to spell words

- a group of campers can be divided into four teams; each team makes their side of the jungle gym into a target challenge for the rest of the group; each group rotates around to try each side

- it's great fun just to put objects into the jungle gym structure at the fastest possible speed; you start with a box of balls or other objects, on "go" we time how long it takes to get all of the balls inside (the balls must remain inside the jungle gym); then you can add the additional timed challenge of having campers climb into the structure and get all of the balls back outside and into the original box

- you can also have some team members inside the structure and some outside, each with an equal number of soft balls or objects; on "go," the people inside try to toss things out of the jungle gym and the people outside try to put them back in; at the conclusion of the time period, we count to see if there are more objects in or out

- have everyone tie as many "monkey tails" (short pieces of rope) to the bars (one per bar) within an allotted time period; to motivate the learning of some knot-tying skills, you can require specific knots, or give different points for different types of knots

- children of every age love to burst through things, so one very cool activity is to cover part of the jungle gym with paper and then let the kids toss things through the paper

## The Swings

☐ teamwork is built through "synchronized swinging"; this can be attempted by connecting all of the swings with horizontal pieces of masking tape and seeing if campers can swing together without breaking the tape

☐ there are many fast, easy, and wonderful ways to make swings into terrific targets—and of course the best thing is that these targets are *moveable*

☐ use masking or duct tape from chain to chain to make squares, rectangles, and triangles (two parallel, horizontal pieces, one above the other, then two more diagonally that come up from the bottom one and meet in the center of the top one) to throw balls, flying discs, and other objects through without breaking the tape

☐ using those shapes again, have one partner in front of the swing and the other behind it; they try to toss the ball back and forth through the taped shapes without breaking any tape; we can push the swing side to side or back and forth to make this more challenging

☐ nothing can compete with the kick kids get out of knocking over things with liquid in them; put paper cups filled with water on the swing seats; a little bit of duct tape on the bottom of the cup will help balance them; balls or bean bags are thrown at the cup to knock it off the seat; we can change the rules to allow striking the chains, or to *require* striking the chains (i.e. no direct hits on the cup), or not to allow any chain contact at all; of course other targets can be balanced or affixed to the seats as well

☐ if we have a tire swing, then we've got even more fun opportunities, including putting a tape grid across the opening to make it harder to toss a ball into or through the swinging tire without breaking the tape

## Monkey Bars

- ☐   these come in various types; most simply they are horizontal ladders on which kids swing from rung to rung to get from one end of the ladder to the other

- ☐   it's fun to hang targets of different sizes and types from the rungs at varying heights (wiffle balls are easy because they already have holes); campers throw stuff at the targets; of course, anything that makes a mess or a splash makes the best target, so water balloons are terrific

## Safety

When we make unusual uses of equipment and brainstorm about creative changes, we must always keep safety in mind. Sometimes these judgments are easy. Doing soccer barefoot with a bowling ball, for example, would be fun, but only briefly.

It might be helpful if I let you know some items that I thought of including on the lists but decided to omit because they may pose unnecessary risks.

First, please note that when objects are tossed at or through targets, we need to use soft objects. I thought about using footballs to throw through the holes in jungle gyms, but I would do so only after considering the age of the campers and weighing the possibilities of balls bouncing back and hitting someone in the face. Similarly, when campers are inside the structure tossing objects out while others are tossing objects in, footballs are not good because they would be thrown at people who might not be prepared to catch them.

There were many instances in which I thought of blindfolding campers to make activities more challenging, but I eliminated these because the risk of injury greatly increases whenever we remove someone's sight.

I thought it might be fun to toss things to a camper who is at the top of a slide or a jungle gym, but I eliminated this because one or both of that camper's hands would be busy doing something other than holding on.

The lesson here is that just as we must be creative in coming up with interesting changes, *we must also be creative in imagining possible safety concerns*. We deal more with this issue when talking about Path 6, which directly concerns keeping things safe.

## So How Do We Introduce These Ideas to Staff?

It's much easier to make creative suggestions to staff when we've already set up the expectation that we will be doing this as a regular part of camp.

Staff should be told during orientation that being creative in our program leadership is not just encouraged, but required. This should be communicated in a positive way, stressing that using creativity is one of the best parts of the job. The relationship between predictability and boredom should be explained. The importance of contrast, surprise, and doing the unexpected should be also stressed. Staff should be given an opportunity to practice creativity by applying the two-question creative approach that we've discussed in this chapter. Safety issues must be discussed, with some specific examples so that staff always keep risk management in mind.

The director then tells staff that one of the supervisors' most important jobs is to help support this creativity by serving as a resource for new ideas and approaches. Staff are told that after the first few days, when everyone has pretty much settled into their schedule, supervisors will be approaching groups and asking them to try out some new ways of doing things. These can be called "experiments" or given some other name. The director points out that these experiments—new or different ways of trying things—are not being suggested because staff aren't doing a good job. They are presented as part of a continual process of keeping things fresh. Staff should be urged to try creating twists themselves.

## What to Say to Staff

Supervisors should reinforce the above points when speaking directly to their individual units before the children arrive.

When I first started as a supervisor, I found that most staff welcomed suggestions and new ideas and were happy to let me work with them and their group to try stuff out. But there were also some staff that seemed less open. This may have been due to ego, defensiveness, or other causes. I wanted to find a way to defuse potential negative feelings from the very beginning of camp, and I found a way to do this that I hope you will find useful.

Basically, I gave a quick little "speech" to the people I was supervising in which I explained that my reasons for visiting their groups had as much to do with me as it did with them.

Here's what I said. You can word it in your own style, but these are the basic "talking points" to get across:

"I'm looking forward to being a supervisor this year. But I'm also a little worried about it, because I don't want to lose touch with the most important reason I like to be at camp—playing with the kids. I miss having my own group.

"So I have a favor to ask. When I walk by your group, please say 'Hi,' and if it's a good time for you, wave me over. Invite me to play or try stuff with you. Depending on what's going on, I may or may not be able to do it right at that moment, but please be open to letting me join your group.

"And I'll tell you another reason that I really hope you'll do this. It's because sometimes it's a little awkward for me to come over to you. I don't want to interrupt what you're doing, and I also don't want you to think I'm trying to breathe down your neck.

"All of the supervisors will be working with all of the groups this summer on thinking up new and fresh ways to do stuff, and so I may come over and ask if we can try an experiment—a creative twist. Please encourage your campers to be positive about this.

"And I want to hear about experiments that you've tried. Not everything may work out, but it's the trying that's really important. We want to spread around good new ideas so that everyone can use them."

## Caution: Change & Age

Our younger campers are so open to trying new and different things. Sadly, as they become older, they may become less comfortable with things that are unfamiliar because they are so concerned about how they will look to others. And, then, of course, they become adults and say things like, "But we've always done it this way."

So please note that some—not all—older campers will resist trying new ways to play games or creative approaches. For some of them, doing something in a new way is threatening to them because they don't know exactly how it works or whether they will be good at it. When you try to play a few minutes of soccer with a variation, for example, some older ones may call this "stupid" and say it's "not regulation."

The best way to handle these campers is gently. These campers need work on skills such as confidence, flexibility, openness, and the ability to try new things without having to be perfect. Smile and tell them that they are right—that this *is* different and creative stuff. Tell them—nicely, warmly, and positively, without lecturing—that creative things are good. They stretch the brain. Say that we may have moments where we don't do things like they do at home in a sports league or in their backyards. At camp, we practice league-type skills, but we go way past that. We also work on being creative, open, and handling change.

Admit that it's easier to do things the way we've always done them. But express confidence in their ability to do hard things. Ask them if they've heard of professional football players who take ballet to learn better balance and control. These players are not wimps. Many professionals introduce variety and special challenges into their workouts to stretch their abilities.

Again, most kids will love the fun and challenge that creative twists bring to camp. But for those who struggle a bit, we just keep our expectations high and support them in becoming more comfortable with doing things in different ways.

## The Way of the Weird

To build a more creative staff culture, show that creativity is valued by paying lots of positive attention to efforts to keep camp fresh. Give special recognition for creativity. Begin a camp tradition: "The Way of the Weird" award. It's to be given to anyone that comes up with a creative way to bring freshness to a camp routine or activity. Find or make an unusual object to serve as a traveling trophy. "Bronzed" (gold spray-painted) rubber chickens make great ones. Gold-sprayed jumbo pretzels are a nice play on the word "twist." Design a special sticker or ribbon that can be given out to a staff person or to her or his group. Be sure to talk about new ideas at staff meetings so these twists can be shared. Make announcements at opening and closing gatherings or meals about unique changes that groups have discovered.

Please do not make this a competition between staff. If we are doing our job right, every staff person should be getting noticed for doing things in creative ways. Some staff will need our help more than others, but every group we supervise should be experimenting with new and exciting ways to make camp a truly unique place.

## Chapter Six

# Praise Positive Staff Behavior

Two summers ago I made a note in a file about an experience at a camp, knowing as soon as I did so that it would serve as the perfect summary of Path 2. Here's what happened: I was doing a follow-up visit at a day camp. I was walking the Paths with a staff supervisor (we'll say it was "Kim") and I asked how a particular counselor was doing. We'd worked with this counselor on some behavior management techniques a few weeks earlier. Kim said, "You know, I think he really gets it now. There haven't been any problems for about two weeks."

I said that was great to hear. And then I asked the key Path 2 question: "Do you think the counselor knows that?" Kim said, "Knows what?" I said, "Knows that you think he's got it and that he's doing a better job?"

Kim paused. "I don't know. I haven't had to talk to him about his group for a while, so I suppose he knows."

I stayed quiet for a moment. This is a very hard thing to do for a person who is paid to talk. But I wanted Kim to think this through. And Kim did—it only took a few seconds.

Kim looked at me and said, "I suppose I should tell him."

## What's in the News?

I would like you to make a guess about something. Here's the situation. Pat, a counselor, is at a climbing wall with a group of campers. We're Pat's supervisor. We walk over to Pat, smile, and say hello. Pat says hello back to us. We say hi to the campers and ask them how they're doing. They chat with us for a few seconds and say things are good. We then turn to Pat and say, with a pleasant expression on our face, "Hey, listen, Pat, do you have a moment? There's something I'd like to talk to you about."

So here's the question: At this moment, is Pat expecting good news or bad?

Over many years of presenting trainings, I've posed this situation and question to many thousands of people, including not only supervisors but the people they are supervising—in other words, getting both sides of the picture. The answer is always the same. *Always*. They guess "bad news." Is that what you wrote? Even if you would have answered differently as a result of your own personal experiences, it's very important to know that everyone else in the universe would have answered in the opposite way.

Now here's the key question: *why* are people so sure about the answer? In my hypothetical, I didn't say what we wanted to talk to Pat about. It might have been about a cool part that we wanted Pat to play in the upcoming special event. It might have been to pass along a compliment from a grateful parent. Our manner and facial expressions were pleasant. We didn't walk up swinging a sharp four-foot sword over our head. So why is it that we can so confidently predict that when a boss asks us if we "have a moment," the odds are overwhelming that this is not to bring us good news?

When I've asked people this question, they've always replied that it's just simply a result of their past experience. Out of the many tales I've heard in my travels, this is one of my favorite demonstrations of this point:

## I Come Not to Be Buried but to Praise...

I was doing a workshop in Florida on management techniques for people who work in social services. During a break, a man came up and explained that in his prior job he had been a supervisor of maintenance crews for the phone company. There had been a particularly brutal heat wave and he decided to do something he hadn't done very often, which was to go to one of the underground cable repair sites and give some support to one of the crews. He drove up, got out of his car, and walked up to the shirtless foreman, who like the rest of the men, was sweating heavily. The supervisor asked how things were going, made pleasant small talk for a few moments, and then said he just wanted to let the foreman know that he and his crew were doing great work, especially under the circumstances. The big-muscled foreman stared at the supervisor and said, leaning on his shovel: "Who said that we weren't?"

The supervisor, taken aback, said that no one had said that. He said again that the crew was doing fine. At this point, the entire crew was slowly walking over and circling around the supervisor with their shovels and pick axes as the foreman asked the supervisor again exactly what he meant. "What was going on?" they all wanted to know. The supervisor sputtered some more about everything being fine, that he hadn't meant anything, or rather that he *had* meant something—that they were doing a great job. The supervisor told me that, for a moment, he felt that he was going to be buried with a phone cable and never seen again. "I couldn't wait to get back into my car and get out of there."

I asked him what he thought had caused their reaction. He said that as he drove back to the office he tried to make a balance sheet in his head of how often he had spoken to his crews solely for the purpose of praising them. "If you'd asked me before that incident I would have said that I did it all of the time. But as I thought about it and really made myself count it all up, I realized that it wasn't as often as I had believed. And when I *was* being positive with them, a lot of the times it was because I also had some stuff that was not so good to talk about."

## The Problem with Sandwiches

The supervisor was speaking here about what I've often heard referred to as the "sandwich." Many supervisors have been taught that the way to speak to employees about negative things is to present it sandwiched between positive things. So in workshops, the trainers instruct supervisors to give a compliment, present a criticism or correction, and then close with a positive comment. I've asked huge numbers of people how they feel about this approach and I've come to the conclusion that this sandwich is mostly baloney.

Even if people feel that the praise is sincere—and my discussions with many different groups about this have convinced me that in a large majority of cases they do not—the problem is that by tying positive comments to the negative stuff, people become suspicious or tense about positive comments *even if they are made without any accompanying negative comments.* In a way, people have become "conditioned" to wait for the "but." Or, as I like to say, when staff see our smiling, sunshiny face come around the corner, they know that the but, if you'll pardon the expression, won't be far behind.

> Here's a nice sandwich: "Fred, I want you to know that I admire and value the amount of enthusiasm and sheer energy that you put into everything you do here. (positive) You just threw a steel chair at me in anger. You must learn to control your temper. (negative) But your aim and follow-through were excellent.... (positive)"

To be fair, the intent of the sandwich is a smart one. It's just an attempt to be tactful and sensitive about people's feelings. But the problem is that too many supervisors present the majority of their praise in moments when the real business at hand is solving a problem or correcting undesired behavior. In effect, they store up some positives in their head and then wait to present them until these corrective moments arise.

Here's what I believe we need to remember at camp: *Praise should not be used primarily as a cushion for what we really want to say.* Path 2 requires us to look at ourselves and monitor on a daily basis what we talk to staff about and why. We don't need an exact ledger, but we do need to raise our self-awareness.

Remember the "balance sheet" in the phone company supervisor's head? That is exactly the right picture for us to use. Great supervisors ask, "What is the balance of our communication about positive things compared to our communication about negative things or things that we want changed?" When our talk about negatives (including sandwiched negatives) so outweighs our talk about positives, we have what I call the *balance problem.*

## The Balance Problem

Here's a fast way to explain why the balance problem *is* a problem. A nurse in California once told me at a workshop I presented that she had just yesterday received her six-month review from her supervisor. She shook her head in a way that said this had not been a very good experience. The nurse said to me, "My boss started by saying that I had improved on many things since the last review." Since this seemed to be a positive thing, I didn't quite get why she was looking sort of sad, so I asked her, "Well, great— so what were some of the positive things that your boss said?" The nurse said—and I will never forget this—"*I don't remember.*"

I was startled by that. The review had only been 24 hours ago. I said, "Well you must remember some of it. What did she say?"

The nurse then said something that should be printed on a plastic card and carried around by every supervisor, every day. She said, *"You know, I was so worried about whatever negatives or criticisms my boss was going to say that I really couldn't pay attention to any of the good stuff."*

## The Need for Praise

The people we supervise need to hear about what they are doing right. They need to hear this so that they know that they are appreciated. They need to hear this so that they feel affirmed and will continue to do even more of the behaviors that we value. They need to hear this because it builds trust between us and helps build a warm relationship instead of a cold one. It motivates.

I sometimes ask in workshops, "How many of you have worked for someone, or had a teacher or a coach or a parent, whose philosophy of leadership was this: 'Look, if my people don't hear from me, then they know everything is going OK.'?"

Most of the hands in the room go up. We then make a list of the negative effects of this type of leadership.

It would be helpful if you would take just a moment and do that yourself now. Write some of them down. There's no right or wrong answer to this. Just jot down some negative effects of the "balance problem"—of communication that is tied more to negatives than positives.

When supervising camp staff, I admit that I sometimes assumed—incorrectly—that many senior, veteran staff didn't need to be praised much because they clearly knew that they were experienced and highly skilled and that others looked up to them. The better they did their job, the less correction they required, so my interaction with them decreased simply because I thought I didn't "need" to speak with them. But of course I did. I came to realize that people who do excellent work, even veterans, need as much feedback as less experienced staff.

Less feedback often leads to lesser levels of motivation and higher rates of burnout among the people that we would most want to stay.

## So Why Aren't We More Positive?

It's pretty obvious by this point that we have to be sure to get out there on Path 2 and talk to staff about positive behavior.

It's interesting to ask at this point, "Why don't more supervisors do that? Why isn't there more positive communication to staff?"

I used to believe that the reason supervisors don't praise staff is because supervision is perceived to be essentially a "fire-fighting" kind of job where we are mostly busy responding to problems.

I was wrong.

This is the single most important thing that I've ever learned about communication. If this were a pop-up book, here's where I'd go three dimensional:

*The main reason that supervisors don't talk as much about positive staff behavior as they do about negative staff behavior is simply because they don't have as clear a picture of what positive staff behavior actually is.*

I've researched this question for over 20 years. I've asked supervisors to make two lists. One list is what they want the people they are supervising to do—positive things that they want to see. The second list is what they want them not to do—negative things that they don't want to see. Then we compare the two lists. The negative list is invariably more specific than the positive list. The negative list is filled with things that people say or do, like "talking behind others' backs," and "being late," and "yelling when they are angry," and "saying 'It's not my job to do that....'"

But the positive list mostly states generalities. It states characteristics or qualities, such as "cooperation" and "flexible" and "hard-working" and "responsible." If there are specific entries on the positive list, most often they are specific things from the negative list with words like "don't..." or "no..." preceding them. In other words, they are not really positives, but the absence of negatives.

A good summary is to say that the negative list has things that people *do*, but the positive list has things that people *are*.

But this is the most interesting part. We are usually *unaware* that we are being more vague with the positives. What I've discovered by having thousands of people make these lists is that people tend to believe that they *are* being specific with the positive list, even though what they are listing are *conclusions* that we draw from people's behavior and not the behavior itself.

For example, when we say that we want staff to be "responsible," that isn't something specific that we can see or hear. Being specific means breaking down the quality "responsible" into the things that we see staff do or say that cause us to *conclude* or *believe* that they are being responsible.

For example:

- ☐   They say, "What can I do to help?"

- ☐   They show up on time, sometimes even a little early.

- ☐   They ask if there is anything they can do to improve.

- ☐   They say, "I need help..." or "I'm not sure what I'm supposed to do...."

- ☐   They tell us if something isn't going right or if they've made a mistake, even when we wouldn't have known unless they told us.

- ☐   When campers don't want to follow rules, they ask the campers to think about what good choices are available when we don't like rules; they have the campers practice figuring out what options they might have besides just ignoring the rules.

It's *these* things—the things that we actually see or hear staff do or say—that are specific.

## The Importance of Being Specific

OK, so what? What's the big deal about being more specific? So we're more vague about positives. Why should we care?

The first reason is that *when we know what we are looking for, we are more likely to see it*. So when we have specific pictures in our head of what positive staff behavior is, it is much easier to find things to praise.

The second reason is that being specific is what makes praise credible.

Remember the phone crew? Suspicious. Searching for ulterior motives. They stood around asking themselves, "OK, what does this guy *really* want?"

Please consider another example:

This is approach number one: I'm a camp supervisor. I go up to Carrie, an arts and crafts assistant instructor, and say, "Carrie, you're doing a terrific job. Great work. Thanks, we really appreciate it."

OK. Not bad. I provided praise. But there's a far more powerful way I could have done it. Let's rewind the tape and try again. Here's approach number two:

This time, instead of telling the staff person that she is good, I tell her *why* she is good. I say out loud what I've seen or heard that has made me conclude that she is doing great work. I say, "Carrie, you know most of these kids' names. We've only been here a week. This really helps kids feel like you know them. That's what great teachers do. Thanks."

Be Carrie for a moment, please. Which of the two approaches described above would mean the most to you? Which one would you believe was sincere, and not just "back-patting" to keep you "motivated" so that you will remain standing in 110 degree heat while small children glue their hands into your hair? Which one do you believe would most show that you are really appreciated?

Right, the first one.

No, of course not the first one. I'm just checking to be sure that you're actually reading this stuff. It's the second one. It was much more credible. Why? Because it was *specific*.

The second approach followed what I call:

## The Law of Positive Communication

The Law of Positive Communication states:

> It's not enough to tell people that they are
> good. We must tell them why.

Telling people why they are good is what makes praise truly effective. What happens when we follow the Law and provide specific praise?

1.  It shows more sincerity, effort, and real appreciation on our part if we actually explain why we are saying it.

2.  People with low self-confidence frequently deny compliments. Specific compliments are harder to deny because they state observed facts.

3.  When people know why we believe they are good, they are more likely to believe it themselves, which builds confidence and positive self-images.

4.  It lets people know specifically what we value so that they will do more of it. (If we just say "good job" then it's harder for them to know what they should continue to do.)

5.  When staff overhear us providing specific praise to others, it is easier for them to discover what we value and begin doing these things themselves. If we just say, "Chris, you're the best!" then they don't know what to do other than change themselves into Chris, which is not a very easy thing to do in these days of increasingly limited medical insurance coverage. Also, general praise can lead to resentment. Remember teachers' pets?

    □  What staff hear: "Jo, you're great. Jo, you're terrific! Jo, you're super!"

    □  What staff think: "Oh, Jo, you're *so* super! Let's shove you off the top of a tall building and see if you can *fly*...."

6.  It makes it easier for us to know what to say when we praise people. We can say what we've just seen or heard—the content comes from what's going on right in front of us, right now.

## Praising Right Away

I've learned that our communication about negative things is generally much faster than our communication about positive things. Sometimes we have a perfect excuse for this. For example, if we don't say something right away when we see a junior counselor violating camp rules by climbing a tree, limbs might get broken—human as well as maple.

But the question to ask ourselves is this: When we see another junior counselor five minutes later, leading campers in a boisterous cheer as they move to their next activity, do we go right over and praise that j.c.? Or do we wait until we see her or him at the end of the day? Or the next morning? Or do we just make a mental note: "Hey, now that's a great junior counselor," but not say it out loud?

Big, basic, important rule from psychology: there's behavior, and there's response. The closer in time the response is to the behavior, the greater the effect that response has on the behavior.

Translation: *be faster.* Praise people as soon as possible. We've been conditioned to believe that saying good stuff to people "can wait" because it's not an emergency. Don't wait. *The best supervisors maximize the power of praise by responding as soon as possible to things that they value.*

## The Benefit of Creating a Positive Atmosphere

If we increase the amount of positive communication with staff, they become more comfortable when we walk up to them and won't necessarily expect "bad news."

Will we still need to speak with staff about negative things— mistakes, unacceptable behavior, and so on? Sure. Path 4 is devoted entirely to that. But if we've been speaking all along with staff about what we value, then when we do need to speak with them about things that are to be corrected, we have a much more trusting and positive context in which to do this.

## Kids, Too

When we increase the amount of positive communication and model how to effectively present specific and immediate praise, we are modeling for staff how they should talk to their campers.

Everything we've said about praise in this chapter applies equally to the way all of us should communicate with children about their behavior. Following the Law of Positive Communication— going beyond "good job!" and saying *why* kids are good—is an enormously effective way to grow terrific behavior in campers.

## What if There's Nothing Good to Talk to Some Staff About?

All staff make good choices every day. As our grandparents reminded us with this clever proverb, "Even a broken clock is right twice a day."

Spotting the one or two small flowers in a garden that is overgrown with weeds can be hard, but the key to success is knowing what flowers look like.

## Coming around the Bend on This Path....

Chapter Seven will help with this behavioral botany by helping us to identify lots of examples of specific and positive staff behavior.

Then, in Chapter Eight, we'll talk about methods to praise the positive behavior of staff in fun, creative ways.

## Our Path 2 Pledge

In summary, there are three things we can do in our work on Path 2. We will work hard to:

1. talk more about what we value, and not just about what we don't

2. make that talk more specific

3. make that talk more immediate

## Chapter Seven

# An Excellent Boss Always Knows the SOSS

Our goal for this chapter is to practice being more specific when we say that a staff person is doing a "good job." We said in the last chapter that the number one reason why supervisors communicate more about negative behavior than positive is because they don't have a specific picture of what positive staff behavior is. We can fix this problem, starting right now.

*Please remember our maxim:* When we know what we're looking for, we're going to see more of it.

## SOSS

I call the positive staff behavior that we're looking for, "SOSS." I pronounce it "sauce" and the four letters stand for: "Signs of Super Staff." Put simply, SOSS are the things that we want staff to do and say when working with campers and with each other. They represent our expectations.

The ingredients of some sauces are well-kept secrets. The job of a superb supervisor is to discover the ingredients that make up outstanding camp leadership. These ingredients are SOSS.

There's only one way I know to learn how to be more specific about skills. We have to practice. We can do this practice together.

## Rating Robin

It is early July and the summer has been going great. The weather has been perfect, the changes in special events this year have been spectacular successes, and the children are having fun. We've only had to send one person home so far. Unfortunately, it was an assistant director. These things happen....

It is late in the afternoon and you are having a conversation with the camp director, T. T asks you if you have any superstars in your unit—leaders that stand out way above anyone else. You say yes, there are several really first-rate people. You add that there is one in particular, Robin, that is just brilliant. This is a new staff person that T does not know well.

T asks you why you believe that Robin is so great. You reply, "Hmm, good question...." which compliments your boss (good move) and gives you a few moments of stalling time to figure out what to say (even better move).

And then, in a moment of well-deserved good fortune—your reward for years of clean living—the phone rings and it's for the director. This gives you a few minutes more to think about how you will answer the question.

So you think about Robin. You need specifics. What have you observed Robin do? What have you heard Robin say? You've had many chances to watch Robin teach as an instructor, run many different kinds of activities as a group leader, be up in front of the entire camp as a participant in special events, and interact with other staff as a member of this camp unit.

The first thing you think of is, "Robin relates really well with the kids, on their level." OK, that's good.

But suddenly your brain is flooded with warm light. You remember reading a riveting book called *Super Staff SuperVision*. You remember not eating or sleeping for days, holed up in a small room with a locked door and unplugged phone, unable to put the book down, your best friends summoning paramedics in concern for your health.

And you remember one part of the book best, where the

author focused on the importance of being specific. The book said that when we *think* we're being specific, we are often just stating general conclusions that are based on things that we've seen or heard. It's those more *specific* things that we're really looking for.

You remember the feeling you had when you read these words, as the sound of bullhorns roared through your shaded window ("Come out—we know you're in there! It's just a book! You must get on with your life. *It's just a book....!!!*). An epiphany of understanding rushed into your mind. So you ran to the bookshelf, looked up "epiphany" in the dictionary, and then shouted out loud to yourself:

"Of course! The value of being specific is that it will make it easier for me to spot this great stuff when others do it. *And if it's easier to spot, then it will be easier for me to tell people that it's good—and why.* And it will also help me teach people how to be better leaders and teachers because I will actually know what the best leaders and teachers do and say!"

Now you look around you. You realize you're back in the camp office. T is still on the phone. You have to answer T's question. So you think about "relates well to kids on their own level" and you ask yourself the right question: *"How do I know?"* What is it that Robin does or says that makes me believe or conclude that Robin is relating to kids on their level?

And having asked the right question, the answers start to flow: You've noticed that:

- ☐ when Robin talks to campers, Robin often bends down or sits down on the ground to speak with them face-to-face.
- ☐ Robin makes lots of eye contact with the kids.
- ☐ Robin learned and used the kids' names right away.
- ☐ Robin really listens to the campers.

## Red Alert!

Oops. Hold on. You're getting good at this specific stuff—you've noticed that this last item, "Listens to the campers," is actually a *conclusion*. In other words, *there are things that Robin does or says* that make you believe that Robin is really listening. What are those things?

47

You picture those moments when you've seen Robin listening. You play the video in your head. What are you seeing and hearing?

- ☐ Robin often repeats what kids say to show that they've been heard or to give them words that help express how they are feeling. So, for example, when one of them says angrily, "Not fair! You didn't make *them* clean up!" Robin says, "You think that you're being treated differently."

- ☐ Robin encourages kids to practice communicating by frequently inviting campers to say more. When one of them says, "Yeah, ropes are my favorite!" instead of saying "Well, I can see that...." and moving on to another subject, Robin smiles and says, "Tell me why that is...." In fact, "Tell me about that..." and "Tell me..." are the most frequent phrases that Robin uses.

- ☐ Robin makes time just to talk with the campers, and makes sure that there are lots of conversations throughout the day about a variety of things, not just behavior management issues. When they are waiting with other groups to go in for a meal or for an event to begin, Robin sits with kids and makes conversation, asking them about all sorts of stuff that the kids care about, showing interest by asking follow-up questions.

- ☐ Robin remembers what the kids have said about their interests and refers back to these things to help make the campers feel like they are individuals who are unique and understood.

- ☐ Robin shows affectionate admiration for the campers by bragging about them to you whenever you come by; and, you've noted, the praise Robin gives is very specific—not "this is the best group" but instead things like, "You know, when I ask our group to clean up, I've gotta tell ya, nobody's faster, and they do it the first time I ask. You've really gotta be there to see it yourself to actually appreciate the speed...."

Your thoughts are interrupted. The director is now off the phone and plops back into the chair next to you. "Sorry about that. Oh, yeah, Robin. Tell me about Robin...."

And now you can. And you do. You are confident. You are specific. You are immortal.

## The "X Is Xcellent" Activity

I've made up an activity to help supervisors identify SOSS and get a very specific picture of exactly what we're looking for. I would appreciate it if you would try it now. Here's how it works. I make some statements about staff, and then you ask, "How do we know?"

So for example, I say, "X is one of our most excellent instructors." You ask, "How do we know?" And when you ask this question, you try to picture a person or persons who are among the very best instructors that you have ever known, and ask the "see/hear" sub-questions we've been using all along: "What does X do or say that makes us so convinced that X is a top teacher?"

Here are some tips:

1.  Without doubt, the biggest secret to making this work—and, frankly, the one thing that almost everyone forgets to do—is to start by visualizing a real person as "X." It is so much easier when you can "run tape" in your head and think about what you've actually observed instead of trying to do this as a theoretical exercise. So, instead of asking yourself, "What do great teachers do?" you want to be sure to ask yourself first, "OK, so who were my best teachers at camp? Who were my best teachers at school?" Picture these people and you're on your way.

2.  Please don't try to do this in your head. Write stuff down. Please. I've done this type of activity many, many times in workshops and we've learned that you only get the full potential benefit if you write.

3.  You already know this stuff. Please trust me on this. You may not be used to being specific about what you've observed, but if you picture people you've known or worked with, you've got what you need to identify great skills.

4.  Everything you write down should be something that a person can do, not be. It should be things that you can walk down the Path and see or hear.

5.  What if you realize that you've listed something that isn't specific? First, give yourself bonus points because it's skillful to notice that it's not specific. Write the general thing down anyway, and underneath it try to break it down into some specifics. Or come back to it later.

6.  A common pitfall is to describe what a staff person does *not* do. So for example we might write, "X doesn't insult campers when they get something wrong" or "X never yells at the kids." It's OK to write these down. Just remember that our goal is to do more than define what is good by the absence of bad. Once written, try to cross these items out and replace them with what X *does* do instead. For example, "When kids get something wrong, X says, 'OK, that's not it, but good try. Let's try again; we can get this....' or "When X gets angry or when the kids do something bad, X stands really still, or crouches down. X gets very quiet, takes a loud deep breath, and talks slowly and quietly. All these things show the campers that they've messed up and that this is serious...."

7.  Please don't worry at all about whether a specific item fits best under one Xcellent category or another. In other words, don't be concerned whether "makes eye contact" fits best under "Xcellent teaching" or "Xcellent communication" or elsewhere. Actually, "eye contact," like many other things you will think of, belongs in more than one category. We are much less concerned with "classifying" these specific skills than just knowing what they are.

8.  How many items should you write down for each category? You have to decide that for yourself, of course. There are hundreds of answers to the "How do we know?" questions. We don't need to know all of them. We could spend the entire camp season—indeed, our entire lives—observing skilled people and adding more specific items to our list. For now, I think that if you work on

coming up with about five, you're doing great. You can consult the examples I've provided in the Liver ("SOSS: Xcellent Xamples") and they may stimulate you to think of more.

"Wait a minute," you say. "Hold on. There are *examples*? You mean *answers*?" Yes, over 150. But as I said in Chapter Five when we were practicing creative twists, if you look at the examples now, then you won't get any practice yourself, and practice is important if we really want to get good at this "being specific" stuff.

## Time to Practice

Below is a list of Xcellent qualities found in super staff. There are others we could add, but I've selected these particular ones because they provide terrific opportunities for practicing identification of SOSS skills.

For each one, please write down answers to the "How do we know?" question by listing as many specific things as possible that a staff person could do or say that would make you believe that she or he had that quality.

1.  X is Xcellent at *group leadership* (How do we know?)

2.  X is Xcellent at *teaching/instructing* (How do we know?)

3.  X is Xcellent at *communicating with campers* (How do we know?)

4.  X is Xcellent at *teamwork with other staff and camp administration* (How do we know?)

5.  X is Xcellent at *being responsible* (How do we know?)

6.  X is Xcellent at *working with camper behavior* (How do we know?)

## How Do We Use This Stuff?

How can the lists of SOSS skills that we've practiced making here and the examples that are supplied as a reference in the Liver help us in our work as supervisors?

These lists can help us:

☐   know what we're looking for so that we can specifically praise staff

☐   identify the skills that we want to teach to others

☐   remind us of the skills that we want to use ourselves when interacting with campers

☐   define excellent staff performance so we can help staff set and reach personal goals

☐   build skill training sessions for orientation; we want to communicate what's on the lists to staff and help them learn these skills

## So...

Would you say that this has been a good chapter? Great. Now, when you say "good," you mean.....?

## Chapter Eight

# Praise In Creative Ways

It always feels good to give someone a compliment. It's one of the best parts of a supervisor's job. Delivering praise can also be fun when it's done creatively. And when creative, it can have an even more powerful effect on staff.

### Noteworthy Praise

All supervisors leave written notes for staff: "Erin—Mrs. Wilford called again this morning and wants to know why Cliff keeps coming home wearing someone else's underwear. Please call her." And: "Rick—Please call a 'Mr. Benton.' He says he is your probation officer. Could I please see you in the office when you get a chance? Thank you."

Remember that you can also use written notes to give praise. They are useful when we don't want to interrupt a staff person, but it is very powerful to leave a note sometimes instead of giving verbal praise. The extra effort it takes to write the brief note is appreciated by staff and can give the praise even greater impact.

When you walk by a swimming instructor who is using some great teaching techniques, try leaving a note describing what you saw or heard that was so good. Ball it up and stick it in the toe of one of the instructor's shoes. When you see a counselor using meal times to have great conversations with campers or to play funny guessing games, sneak a note about this halfway under the counselor's plate at lunch when she or he goes up for seconds.

Have fun with this; be creative. Have a note delivered by a "special messenger. " You can also seal it in an envelope and tape it to a cabin door.

## Praise Staff by Speaking to Their Campers

The counselor of a younger group of girls has been doing a terrific job. Try this, please. Identify a specific reason why you believe the counselor is so terrific. Walk up to her group. Ignore the counselor; talk directly to the kids. Pretend the counselor is not there. Say something like this: "Hey, ladies, how are you doing? That's great. Listen, can I ask you a question? Thanks. Have you seen any counselors here at camp that know all of their campers' names already? You have? Who? Really? How can you be sure—I mean, how do you know this? She uses your name when she talks to you? Every time? Whoa. You know, only the best counselors can do that."

Now turn to the counselor, smile, and thank her. Believe me, she'll appreciate the extra creative effort you put into presenting the praise. And when praise is presented in a package like this, it has maximum impact and is not soon forgotten.

And here's the best part—think about what this does to the relationship between campers and counselor. By putting the campers in a position where they are talking positively about their counselor, it helps build a solid relationship between them and their counselor. Of course, when you do this sort of thing with younger campers, they don't just "talk." They scream and point. They also jump up and down. "It's *our* counselor, it's *our* counselor, it's *our* counselor!"

## Creative Rumors

Here's another example. We're on Path 2 and we see another great staff person. As before, we take a moment to think of a specific reason why we believe that this counselor is so good, and then make the approach. Again, we speak directly to the campers. "Excuse me, gentlemen. You guys look like you're having a great time here; how are you doing? Alright. I want to ask you something. Have you had a chance to watch any of the other groups around here? Have you noticed what kind of games and things they play?" At this point, please be assured that you have the riveted attention of every young man in this group, for the simple reason that they have no idea yet what you're talking about.

You continue: "I heard a rumor." Pause. "I heard that there is a group here at camp—now I'm not saying this is actually true, you understand, because you can't always believe what people say—but I did hear people saying that there was a counselor here who was making up a bunch of different games every day that no one else was playing—games that no one had ever seen before. What? *You* do that? New ones? Well, do me a favor, please, when you see that counselor, would you please tell him that we really appreciate creative people around here. You guys are really pretty lucky...." Now start to walk away. If the children in this group are younger, they will be screaming at you and pulling on your arm, trying to get you to look at their counselor.

## Older Campers

Does this sort of thing work with older groups? Sure, but of course we play it differently. With the older groups we do this with tongue in cheek. We sort of wink at them as we say it to let them know that they are in on the joke. And we make it shorter, without the embellishments that the younger kids love so much.

On occasion, older campers may try to mess with you, acting "contrary" or sarcastic because, sadly, they believe that this is how they have to act to show that they are "grown up." They may declare that the person you are talking about is not their counselor, even though it plainly is. When they do this, I just nod knowingly and tell them that it's very shrewd of them to keep their leader's talents a secret, because otherwise everyone at camp would want to get in their group or steal the counselor for their own group.

In these circumstances, I will sometimes also smile and gently explain to campers that I'm just trying to give their counselor a compliment. Often campers don't really think about how acting "contrary" affects the feelings of others.

## Creative Compliments Create Comfort

Please note that this creative, indirect praise is particularly effective for praising a staff person who has some discomfort about being given a direct compliment. As you build trust with such a person, as they gain confidence in their job, and as you continue to keep your praise specific and informative instead of general and "gushy," she or he will become more comfortable accepting positive comments. In the meantime, please don't miss out on the fun—try this form of creative praise.

## Extra SOSS

Here's another great way to communicate positively about skills that we want to reinforce. Consider having a "Skill of the Day." Pick an item from one of your SOSS lists and post it somewhere that staff will see it as they begin work that morning. Explain to staff that you will be asking them to focus on a special and important skill and urge everyone to remember to make use of it throughout the day.

Some great examples: bending their knees when they speak to campers, doing fun things like tag or word games or follow the leader during transition periods, and so on. Tell staff that all supervisors will be looking out for the skill and will give a thumbs up or high five when they see it. By focusing on a single important skill, it makes it easy to recognize the skill and provide praise throughout the day when you notice people making the effort to use it.

This is a great way of following up on skills presented during orientation. It can also be used to introduce new skills as the season progresses.

## Chapter Nine

# Support Staff & Help Them Grow

We've already stated in Chapter Three that the most important role of a boss is to provide support for staff. Although we provide such support by walking all six Paths, on this particular path it is our special focus.

## The Big Question That All Staff Ask About Supervisors

We tell staff: "We care about you."

But one of the most important things for supervisors to remember is this:

"Talk is cheap." What matters least to staff is what we say. What matters most is what we do. When we say we care, do staff believe us? In other words, the key issue is credibility.

Every staff person silently asks the following question, and every supervisor needs to know that it is being asked:

*What evidence do I have that my supervisor actually cares about me and my work?*

## Defining P.O.S.

The answer to the above question is what I call P.O.S., which stands for *proof of support*. Proof of support is the *credible* evidence that we provide to staff that we genuinely care about them and their work.

Staff have several follow-up questions that they then ask:

☐    When was the last time I saw proof of support?

☐    How often does proof of support appear?

☐    What triggers or prompts the appearance of a supervisor's support? For example, when a staff member messes up, we may suddenly see 80 supervisors "hovering" to keep an eye on what's going on. Do positive events trigger support, or does a staff member have to do something wrong to get all of this additional attention?

## Providing P.O.S.

I know that it won't shock you at this stage of the book to learn that the word "specific" is going to come flying over this Path at some point. It's that time again.

Please recall from Chapter Six that "specific is credible; general is less credible." The trick to P.O.S. is making sure that we focus on things that we can *do* or *say*, not on things that we can *be*. In other words, we don't want to say, "I'll try to be more responsive." What we want to do is identify some things that we could do or say that would lead someone to believe or conclude that we are more responsive.

Let's look further at this example of responsiveness. Sometimes staff will ask us a question or make a request, and we say that we'll get back to them. Here are three ways of demonstrating P.O.S. in these situations:

1.    First, we need to be sure that we *do* get back to them. We never want to put staff in the position of having to wonder whether to ask us again or cause them to worry that if they do ask, we will become annoyed or feel that they are bothering us.

2.    Second, there is almost no P.O.S. stronger than getting back to a staff person at super speed. We've all had

occasions where we've asked a question in a voice-mail message or an e-mail and the person answered back only minutes later. Since we knew that the person we were hoping to get an answer from was very busy, the promptness of her or his response told us that she or he chose to make our question a priority. As camp supervisors, we can't always give an immediate reply, but we should know that the faster we get back to the staff, the stronger the measure of P.O.S.

I was once consulting and training at a camp mid-summer, when a very slight drizzle began. It lasted only a minute or two and just as people were deciding to move inside to wait it out, the rain stopped. I walked with a supervisor to gymnastics, which was set up outside that day, and I saw one of the instructors wiping off some tumbling mats that were on the ground. She had only one rag and it was quite wet. I asked her the central question of camp supervision: *"Is there anything we can do to help?"*

She smiled and said that it would be great if she could get some dry towels to finish wiping up. The supervisor said "On the way..." and took off running at full speed. The instructor's face showed that she was really impressed. But this expression broadened even more when the supervisor returned, again at a full run, in under 120 seconds, with an armful of towels. She thanked the supervisor and all three of us wiped off mats. I wish there had been a way to measure how many people the gymnastics instructor told about this during the rest of the day. Here, clearly, was a supervisor who knew that *in two minutes a reputation for service and support could be built for no greater cost than one quick sprint.*

3.   Third, when we can't give staff a response because we don't have the information or decision that they requested, it is very important that we give them a "status report" to let them know that we're working on it.

If a counselor's question, for example, requires me to speak to Bruce, but I find out that Bruce will be tied up with something all day and I won't be able to get to him, it's P.O.S. to mention this to the counselor as soon as I learn it. I suspect that the main reason that so many supervisors don't provide these status reports is that all of us hate to say "I don't know yet" or "I'm not finished." But supervisors should know that when we take a few extra moments to let staff know what's going on, staff consider this another solid sign of P.O.S.

Here are a few more ways to demonstrate P.O.S.

☐ Make suggestions to a staff person of creative variations they can use when leading or teaching a particular activity; demonstrate them to the group.

☐ Teach a twenty-questions guessing game to a group that they can play while they are moving from one activity to another.

☐ Take over the leadership of a group for fifteen minutes on a really hot day to give a group leader or instructor a brief break and a chance to recharge.

## The P.O.S. Activity

When I do workshops or retreats for camp supervisors, we do a simple but very powerful activity that is based on the P.O.S. concept. In only fifteen minutes, we can produce a detailed list of dozens of things that we can do right away to provide credible support on Path 3.

I strongly recommend that you first do this activity yourself and then compare notes in a discussion with other supervisors and administrators.

Here's all there is to it:

Please get a piece of paper and take about three to five minutes to write down every possible thing that you can think of that a camp supervisor or other administrator can do to support or respect a staff person or other camp employee or volunteer. Remember, these can't be things that we can BE ("helpful"); they must be things that we can DO or SAY ("teach a game to be used between activities").

## Coming Attractions

As part of our proof of support, we can motivate staff by helping them set and achieve personal goals. We'll discuss this in detail next, in Chapter Ten.

We can also provide guidance and motivation when staff are working with children who present special challenges. We'll identify specific techniques for these situations in Chapter Eleven.

And in Chapter Three Hundred Thirty, we'll reveal how to use automobile odometers to measure the fat content in fast food.

## Chapter Ten

# Highering Staff to Motivate Success

To get people to become part of our staff, we hire them. When we're walking on Path 3, we support staff by helping them to enhance their skills and stay motivated. I call this process *"highering."*

## Growth Is for Staff, Too

We want our campers to experience personal growth at camp. We provide a positive, enriching environment in which they can learn positive things that will help them to become their best.

Now we have to ask ourselves: Don't we expect exactly the same thing for staff? Don't we promise such growth in our recruitment of staff? It's our responsibility as supervisors to do our part in fulfilling that promise.

## Motivation and Perceived Value

Highering staff means helping them to develop in positive ways that they will perceive as valuable. The key word in the last sentence is *"they."* When staff get things that *they* consider to be worth their time and effort, then we can expect them to feel—and report to others—that working at camp is a good deal.

I'm often asked how to best motivate staff. Perhaps the most motivating thing in the world is to know that if we do good work, we will get things that we need and want. We can strongly motivate staff by helping them to reach their personal goals.

## Highering Begins in the Interview

Some potential staff may come to us with a very clear picture of the personal goals that they would like to achieve at camp. Most staff, however, will need our guidance in identifying and prioritizing these goals. We can begin to do this during the job interview.

We use the interviewing process to try to select people whose goals are consistent with the goals of our camp. If the word "party" figures prominently in their list of personal goals, we'll probably take a pass.

In the interview, we want to ask candidates how they want to grow from the camp experience. They will, we hope, talk to us about wanting to make an important contribution to the children. Knowing that one is making a positive difference is an important part of job satisfaction and motivation.

But we want to be sure that we also ask them what they want to get for *themselves*, beyond the great feeling one gets from positively affecting the children. We ask them what skills they'd like to learn or learn to do better as a result of working at camp. We emphasize that these should be skills that the candidates feel would be valuable to them in their own future.

If a person has difficulty identifying specific skills or other goals, we can help them by suggesting some that we can make achievable through the camp experience. But here's a very important technique: to make sure that the candidate is *really* interested in these things—and would therefore be truly motivated by working to achieve them—we must ask follow-up questions. For example, we can ask, "Why would learning that be important to you?" or "What is there about this that you think would make it valuable for you?"

In general, we want to get staff to begin thinking about achieving personal goals right away. Guiding them to do that helps us demonstrate our sincere interest in their development and shows them that we are serious about promoting growth of not only children, but the adults who lead the children.

## Re-Interviewing Returning Staff

I frequently get asked about returning staff—"Should they be interviewed again?" I'll give you my personal feelings about this, respecting that different directors have varying views on this subject. In my opinion, under no circumstances would I ever rehire a person without interviewing them prior to each season.

The type of interview for returning staff will be different, of course, and it can certainly be brief. If we're considering having a person back, then we've already determined their level of qualification based on actual past performance. The purpose of re-interviewing is to determine *current* goals. We don't ever want to assume that a person's goals for one season will be the same for another season. They might be the same, but they might not. It is very important for us to find out why someone would want to return. Is it because they haven't given it much thought and this— a job that they know they can do—is just an easy choice? Or are they really interested in continuing their development as a leader—pushing themselves to an even higher level of performance?

## The Term "Goals & Growth"

I use the term "Goals and Growth" to describe what we are working on when we are highering staff. Here's why. Most staff will see value in developing new and better skills. But some staff—usually those who lack confidence or those who believe they already know everything—get defensive or uncomfortable if we tell them that we want them to get "better" at their job or "improve their skills." They may think, "What are you saying, that I'm not good enough? That I don't know how to do my job?"

I have found "Goals and Growth" to be a more gentle way of saying that at all levels of experience, no matter how good we already are, there are always ways to challenge ourselves more. And when we keep challenging ourselves, we stay motivated as well.

I sometimes refer to the Goals and Growth as "G & G"—I believe that using this informal abbreviation helps keep this process less intimidating and more comfortable for some staff.

## Explaining the Highering Process in Staff Training

I explained in *Training Terrific Staff* how to begin orientation by motivating staff with a clear and powerful identification of goals.

It's important to explain to staff that there are not one but two sets of goals at camp. The first one is helping our campers to grow. In orientation, we ask staff, "What positive differences do we want to see in the children as a result of camp?" The second goal is helping our staff to grow. We ask, "What positive differences do we want to see in ourselves as a result of camp?"

We present to staff three reasons that make working on *staff* Goals and Growth important:

1.  We describe our commitment to making sure that staff not only feel satisfied about what they do for the children's future, but also what they do for their own.

2.  We explain our concerns about burnout and how it is frequently caused by the absence of challenges. Without specific goals for ourselves, we don't have much to reach for, which lowers our motivation and our personal satisfaction with the job.

3.  We explain that if we push ourselves and reach for higher levels of skill, then we are serving as role models for our children. How can we expect children to keep on learning if we've decided that we're not going to continue to learn ourselves?

The director or orientation leader then further explains that supervisors will be meeting with staff as soon as possible to talk to them individually about their G & G plans. The theme is simple: "Everybody, from the director to junior staff, will always be working on G & G, all of the time." Working on G & G means working on skills that we believe will not only be of value to us in our work at camp, but valuable throughout our lives.

We provide time near the beginning of orientation for staff to take a few quiet minutes to write down some things of life-long value that they would like to work on. We tell staff that there are no wrong answers. To help staff do this writing, we can give them a sample list of some important areas for Goals and Growth. Here are a few examples of areas for G & G (camp administrators should, of course, add others that they believe are valuable options at their camp):

- ☐ teaching others
- ☐ listening
- ☐ developing skills to solve challenging problems
- ☐ promoting teamwork
- ☐ presenting in front of groups, both large and small
- ☐ being creative
- ☐ organizing and planning
- ☐ helping children learn to communicate their feelings
- ☐ helping children learn how to solve problems
- ☐ helping children learn how to work in teams and groups
- ☐ helping children to make better choices about their behavior
- ☐ helping children to be more responsible

Staff should be told that the examples on the sheet are intended only to start their thinking. They should be encouraged to write down any of their personal goals, even if they are not listed in one of the examples.

Certainly, all of the items listed above will help staff in their work at camp. But items such as "helping children to communicate their feelings" can be of life-long value to some staff because they intend to continue to work with children or raise children of their own. An item like "developing skills to solve challenging problems" may be of life-long value to staff because they believe problem-solving will be a core skill for advancement in a future profession that might have nothing at all to do with leading children.

Staff should be asked to identify the top two or three G & G areas in which they have the greatest interest, or otherwise prioritize their responses.

We have staff put their names on their Goals and Growth sheets and hand them in. The sheets can be given to the appropriate supervisors and used by them in their later conversations with staff. It's important to explain in a positive way why we are collecting the sheets, particularly so that this does not look or feel like we are collecting "homework papers." We can explain to staff that when we write down our goals and share them with others who can help support us, research shows that we are more likely to reach those goals.

## An Option for Camps with Volunteer Staff

If you are an administrator at a camp staffed with volunteers who walk right off a bus to begin work immediately with your core staff, then please consider sending a Goals and Growth letter to the volunteers before they arrive. You can explain the G & G concepts that we've described in this chapter and ask the volunteers to take a few moments to think about, or write down, some personal goals.

## Short Individual Meetings with Staff

*It is very important for each supervisor to have a brief one-on-one conversation with every staff person they will be supervising, before or at the very start of the first session.*

We need to do everything we can to treat this as an important priority and be creative and persistent in trying to make this happen. It's hard to establish a positive and effective working relationship with someone with whom we've never had even a short conversation.

I can certainly report to you that at every one of the different camps where I worked as a staff person, my only one-on-one conversation with a representative of the camp was with the director during the interview. During orientation, unless I had a question, my only contact with the administration was in group meetings. As best as I can remember, once the campers arrived, my first one-on-one conversations with my supervisors were initiated by me and concerned a problem, a need for a schedule adjustment, or other similar issues. I can't remember the details of any of these conversations, but I can tell you for sure that they were *not* about my personal goals or what valuable things I wanted to get out of my work at camp.

I believe it would have been better if there had been a chance, however brief, to meet and speak with the person who was going to be my direct boss before I began leading campers.

In fact, I hope that you would agree that where there is such an initial introductory conversation, it probably increases the chances that a staff person will ask a question or ask for help during those often hectic first days of the first session and throughout the season. As we know, sometimes staff don't speak up because they are afraid of looking stupid or weak. If the beginnings of a positive and respectful relationship between supervisor and staff person are in place, this will increase trust, which in turn makes it easier for staff to communicate about things that might be hard to talk about.

("Um, Terry, I'm Michael Brandwein, with the Wounded Beagles group, second grade boys, and uh, I have a kid in my group who keeps shouting that he's really going into third grade, because his parents decided to skip him ahead but forgot to tell camp; and he does look older and bigger than the other boys, although maybe that's just a false impression I have because of that long knife he's been carrying....)

## Timing

Ideally, these one-on-one conversations should occur before the campers arrive. At resident camps, it will often be easier to find time for this because we are there 24 hours a day. At day camps and even some resident camps, training time is sometimes more limited and we may need to have these conversations during the first few days of the opening session. In that case, supervisors can try to bring someone with them or work in pairs so that the second person can take the leadership of a group for a few minutes while this conversation with the staff person takes place.

In the absolute worst case scenario, when someone tells me that they believe it is completely impossible to speak to each staff person one-on-one because of the size of staff and the time limitations, then we need to look at the option of speaking with staff in small groups of 2, 3, or 4. Although less personal, this would at least allow *some* initial relationship-building.

## What Should We Talk About?

The supervisor will begin the brief conversation with the staff person with the simple things that start building a relationship, saying things like:

- ☐ "It's nice to be working with you..."
- ☐ "I'm here to support you..."
- ☐ "It's important to me that you feel comfortable coming to me whenever you have a new idea or a question..."
- ☐ "I promise to do whatever possible to help you do your best possible job and have a great season..."

Then the supervisor can refer to the Goals and Growth sheet written by the staff person during orientation as a starting point for discussing her or his goals. This is done in a low-key, warm manner. "It's really important to me that you find working here to be a valuable experience—that you not only help the kids grow and have a great time, but that you also get stuff for yourself from working here. So I just want to talk to you for a few minutes about what you want to get out of this. I'd like both of us to get started thinking about it so that I can do whatever I can to make sure that you reach your goals this summer."

Here's the key secret to asking staff about their personal goals: *just asking the question contributes to relationship-building success, no matter how they answer.* Of course, we hope that they will talk to us and work with us on their goals. But even if a staff person doesn't have a clue what their personal goals are (though they certainly should, since they've spoken about them in their interview and written about them in orientation), our asking the question demonstrates that we care about the staff person.

If we really want to do a stronger job motivating staff and preventing burnout, then we must remember that it is highly motivating for staff to work for people who care about them as *individuals*. People love to be asked: "What do you care about?" and "What do you want to get out of this?" and most importantly, "How can I help you get it?"

## Choosing G & G Skills to Work On

The trick here is to keep the process of working on G & G as simple as possible. Most importantly, we need to recognize that there is no one right way to do this and our efforts should be tailored to each person.

Our role here as supervisors is like a coach, working with each player to achieve a higher level of skills. First, we help the staff person identify a G & G area on which they'd most like to work. They may have already decided this when they did their writing on the Goals and Growth sheet during orientation. If the staff person still isn't sure at this point what goal they want to reach for, we can talk to them about this further and also ask if it's OK for us to suggest something. We might say, for example, "What if we worked on some new ways of being creative with the kids—you know, so they're really motivated and stay interested? That would help make your job easier, and practicing creative stuff is something that we can use for our whole life, right?"

Next, we help the staff person figure out what they can work on that will give them skills in the G & G area that they've chosen. Let's continue with our example of creativity. Creativity means doing things in new and different ways. So here are two examples of things that a staff person could practice that would develop greater creative skills:

1.  The staff person will think of ways to change a game or activity that is familiar to campers to make it more interesting and fun for them, and then teach it to them.

2.  The staff person will make up a new game or activity of her or his own and teach it to the campers.

The staff member can pick one of these two suggested skill items to work on. Then, we just follow-up on important things taught to staff during orientation. We will have already presented training on how to be creative in planning and leading activities (please see Chapter Five), so these G & G's will provide opportunities to practice and use these skills.

## Other Examples of G & G Skills

Suppose the staff person selects (or is guided by us to) the G & G area of "presenting in front of large and small groups." Here are some things in that area that a staff person could work on:

1. learn a song that campers already know and lead a group (first a small one, then perhaps larger ones) in singing it

2. teach and lead a new song that campers do not know

3. read a story to a group of campers

4. tell a story to a group of campers, using a note card

5. tell a story without using any notes

6. make up a story and tell it (which then works on skills from the creativity area as well)

7. play a non-speaking part in a skit or other presentation (which could be as simple as standing with others in the background or doing a simple task while in front of large groups, such as in flagpole ceremonies)

8. play a small speaking part in a skit or other presentation

9. play a big speaking part in a skit or other presentation

10. make up a skit with others or by herself or himself and play a small or big role in it (which again combines practice on creativity skills)

Some of these skills are more challenging than others. For some staff, just being up in front of the whole camp by standing silently (in the back) with a group of other people will be a great accomplishment. Others, with greater comfort and experience, will enhance their skills by jumping into a more advanced level right away.

## How Do I Get More Help with G & G Skills?

Please refer to the Liver in the back of the book, "SOSS: Xcellent Xamples." This section lists over 150 specific skills that staff can work on in a variety of G & G areas.

## Providing Guidance

Once we've identified the target G & G skills, we work with staff to develop them. Our degree of involvement as supervisors will depend on the staff person's level of motivation and skill. Some staff will just work on their chosen G & G skills on their own and keep you posted on what they are doing. For example, a group counselor working on creativity (changing a familiar activity) might invite you over to field hockey to demonstrate some creative variations for pre-game drills. The campers might have duct tape wrapped sticky side up around their sticks and be passing the "puck"—a small ball—directly from one stick to another to work on control and to practice looking around to see who is "open." In such a case, we'd praise the counselor for coming up with not only something unique, but something that helps teach good techniques to the campers. Then we'd encourage the counselor to try variations at some other activity areas and say that we are looking forward to seeing those as well.

## Providing Greater Levels of Guidance: An Example with Creativity

Other staff may need more coaching from us when working on their G & G skills. We might need to visit field hockey and talk through the creative process with staff person Chris while the campers are playing a regular game. We remind Chris that the two key creative questions are "What do the campers expect?" and "How can we mess that up?" The staff person shrugs and has no idea.

So we guide a little more by asking some more specific questions. "Well for a start, let's look just at the goals. How many are there? Right. Now one of the principles of change is messing with the number of things. So instead of having just two goals, what could we do? Yeah, right, we could have more of them, like four. Where would you put the two extra ones? Good, sure, that would work. Let's give that a try. We'll do this together. The idea here is that I'm going to try to present it to them as a challenge, so they feel complimented. How about I explain it to the group to show you what I mean? Is that OK? Great—help me get them all together in the middle here, will you?"

With Chris' help, we gather the campers. Please note how we keep Chris involved and in the "center" of things even though we're taking the lead:

"Hey, you guys, thanks for taking a break for a second. This is really a good game. I was just talking to your counselor, and Chris and I decided that you guys are ready for a challenge. You obviously have got this regular field hockey stuff down, so just as an experiment—and I haven't done this with any group yet, but I think this is the perfect group to try it with—here's what we're going to do.

"Let me ask you a question. How many goals are there now? Right, and anybody can play with two goals. Now check this out: Chris is going to take these four safety cones and place them on both sidelines. Watch. Now how many goals have we got? Right.

"Now Chris is going to do something special with the one on this side. Watch this. How wide is it now? Pretty standard, pretty easy, right? OK, Chris is going to make this harder. Harder would be what, guys, closer together or farther apart? Yeah, that's what Chris is doing. Whoa, that's really close. Chris obviously thinks you guys are good. OK, now we're going to need two more goalies so Chris is going to be one and I'll be the other. Chris, which one looks good to you? Cool, so I'll take this really narrow nightmare one that Chris just made for us on this side. Now, all you guys are staring at me because I know you've got a question: which goal is yours? Here's where it gets good: you can shoot at either one. Both of the side goals are for everybody.

"So let me ask you guys a question: with four goals instead of two, do you expect there to be more action or less action? Right. More practice shooting on the goal or less practice? Yep. This should be awesome. You guys have got a counselor with a wicked imagination here—let's give it a try and see what happens...."

Later, I'll speak with the counselor, compliment Chris on how it went, and point out a few things that will help Chris learn how to do this without me. I'll mention how I motivated the campers to participate by involving them through the asking of questions and also by making statements that made their group and this variation on the activity special; such statements included:

- ☐ you guys are ready for a challenge

- ☐ you've got this regular activity down

- ☐ I haven't done this with a group yet (by the way: I don't say this if it's not true; if I have done it with other groups, I might qualify this by saying I haven't done this with another group in this unit, at this age level, etc.)

- ☐ this is the perfect group to try something hard

- ☐ anybody can do two goals

- ☐ this goal is a narrow nightmare (therefore especially hard)

I'll ask Chris to notice that I didn't ask the campers if they wanted to do any of this. I just sort of swooped in on them. I presumptively presented it as something that, of course, a group of this expert caliber would want to try. I focused on making it so challenging and attractive to them that they didn't really have a chance to say, "This is stupid" or "Why are we doing this?"

I'll also point out how I asked them questions at the end to help them see for themselves that this was not merely fun or silly but something that would give them practice getting even better at something that *they* valued—scoring points. I didn't just lecture this at them. I helped them figure it out by asking them what would happen to their skills if they met the challenge.

So those are options I have in speaking with Chris to help Chris start doing some of this without me. Now I want to speak with you for a moment about how I got Chris involved.

## Involving the Staff Person

When coaching people to learn higher skills, how we speak is as important as what we are saying. So please note the following:

- ☐ I said, "Chris and I decided...." instead of "I thought...." to immediately "attach" Chris to the creative idea, not only in the campers' minds, but also in Chris'.

- ☐ I said, "Chris is going to take these cones...." By saying this, it makes it impossible for Chris to just hang back and watch me "perform" in front of the campers. It would have been easy for me to move the cones myself. But by directing Chris to do it, Chris is brought front and center and it's Chris who is doing the creative thing. I'm just "narrating" it.

☐ Now my favorite part: I have Chris create the really narrow goal. But I don't tell Chris how to do this. I'm actually letting Chris figure this out right in front of the campers. Please listen in again:

"How wide is the goal now—pretty standard, pretty easy, right? OK, *watch Chris make this harder.*"

I don't tell Chris how to do this; I just pause and let Chris think; if Chris doesn't get it, it's easy for me to provide more clues, using my conversation with the campers as a way in which I can guide Chris:

"Harder would be what, guys, closer together or farther apart? Yeah, that's what Chris is doing. Whoa, that's really close. Chris obviously thinks you guys are good...."

☐ I look for opportunities to give Chris some power and control: "Chris, which one (extra goal) looks good to you?"

## Providing Greater Levels of Guidance: An Example with Getting Up In Front of Groups

How could we coach staff to develop skills for "presenting in front of a group?"

☐ We can suggest songs or stories that are at the right level of challenge for a particular staff person.

☐ We can offer to help them find an activity, skit, or other large group event in which they could play a part.

☐ We can offer to rehearse something with them before they do it.

☐ We can offer to go up in front with a staff person and do something as their partner, sharing responsibilities.

☐ We can offer to present something ourselves and then speak with the staff person afterwards about how we did it, why we made certain choices, and so on.

## Praising Success

It's important to do more than let staff know that we are pleased with their accomplishments. And, of course, you will be stunned to hear that this praise should be specific.

A good technique is to ask staff how *they* felt when they tried something new, to give them an opportunity to evaluate what worked well and what might require more practice.

For example, we might say, "Lee, you asked them a ton of questions and they were so ready to show how smart they were. You really had them teaching themselves, figuring out stuff *with* you instead of just listening to someone lecture. How did that feel, using more questions? Did you see differences in how they were responding?"

## How Many G & G's Should a Staff Person Work On?

This is one of those "everybody's different" issues. Some staff will work on skills in more than one G & G area at once, others on one at a time. Some will take a day or two to practice and demonstrate a G & G skill and some may take a week or two. Naturally, the extent to which a staff person works on G & G's will influence our evaluation of this person. Our very best staff are working on their skills all of the time.

The only requirement is that each staff person always be reaching for something. We remind ourselves again here that for the highering process to be motivating, this "something" must be perceived to be of value by the staff person.

## What If There Are Staff Who Aren't Interested in Goals & Growth?

If a staff person shows only a little interest in Goals and Growth, it's our job to build on what little motivation there is and help them find some success in stretching their skills. As they experience even a little success, there will be increased willingness and motivation to do more.

But what if there is no interest at all? What if we try to talk to a staff person about this G & G stuff and they don't seem to care? What if continued growth is of no interest whatsoever to a staff person?

Then we hired them by mistake. Mistakes happen. Our goal is to *hire only people who are interested in being highered.* Sometimes we miss. In this instance, we'll have to do the best we can with what we've got. Most staff will have an interest in reaching goals by learning skills that have value to them.

## The Circle of Motivation

When we help staff "higher themselves" by working on Goals & Growth, we provide important motivation. People don't burn out as frequently when they have challenging and interesting things to reach for that they believe are of value to them.

But highering staff is not just for the benefit of staff. When staff learn higher-level skills, they do an even better job for the campers.

And then it all comes "full circle." Because when campers are better served, staff get even more personal satisfaction from seeing that their work is making a difference, which is one of the most powerful motivations of all.

**Chapter Eleven**

*CORAL –
THIS IS A
CHAPTER WE
SHOULD SIT AND
DISCUSS*

# Supporting Staff Who Are Dealing with Challenging Children

Some children present tough challenges. Their repeated bad behavior and lack of skills in getting along with people can cause us to secretly conclude that the only reason they have been put on Earth is to shorten our life span. These children require greater patience, more expert technique, and lots of extra time.

There are also children who are challenging not because they have bad behavior but because they have special problems or circumstances that demand, again, lots of extra time and attention from staff. There may be a child, for example, who never wants to do anything, or a child who is extremely bright and so focused that it is hard to get this child to make transitions from one activity to another.

I should make clear at the outset that I love these children. They are often the ones in which we can make the biggest difference. Yes, our work with them can be stressful and sometimes stretch us to our limits. But because it is very important to me to become the best possible teacher and leader of children that I can be, I remind myself that the greatest skills are honed by what is difficult, not by what is easy. It's the children who require more effort from us who teach us the most. They cause us to develop stronger skills, which we can then use for the benefit of all children.

When a staff person has one or more challenging children in her or his group, it's our job on Path 3 to provide extra support for two purposes: to help the child or children, and to keep the staff person motivated, dedicated—and alive. In this chapter, we'll identify effective techniques to provide this support.

## Making Expectations Clear

There are four messages that we want to deliver clearly to staff during orientation.

1.  **"We want you to tell us about certain types of situa-tions right away."** There are certain situations which we want staff to inform camp administrators about immedi-ately, so that we can be sure that support is delivered as soon as possible.

    Each camp administration must decide in advance what these situations are. An easy example is when a staff per-son suspects that a child is a victim of abuse. But other examples might include an unusual degree of homesick-ness or repeated refusals to participate in activities.

    Our key responsibility here is to provide specific guidelines so that staff don't have to guess about when to speak to a supervisor in these more serious situations. For example, when we say "unusual" homesickness, we could tell staff that any time a child shows signs of homesickness for more than X days, tell a supervisor. "Repeated" refusals to participate can be defined with a specific number; some camps tell staff that any time the refused activity is swim-ming, an administrator must be informed even if this happens only once. How we define these things will be up to each camp. The important requirement is to be sure that staff know exactly what we expect.

2. **"This is who you should speak to...."** In most cases we will want staff to speak to their direct supervisor. If that supervisor is not available, however, we need to decide what we want a staff member to do. Are there instances where we might want a staff person to immediately inform the office and leave a message for a director or assistant director? Again, these policies are to be decided by each camp; thinking about these things before orientation is important.

3. **"Asking for help is smart."** We must tell staff that if they ask for help or support (using the method we will teach them—please see below), we believe that this is professional behavior which is highly valued at our camp. Some staff may be afraid that if they bring a challenging situation to the attention of a supervisor, the supervisor may think that they are weak, unqualified, unintelligent, inexperienced, lazy, or worse. We must anticipate these apprehensions by stating them out loud and explain clearly and warmly that we do not have such negative thoughts, and that in fact we greatly value prompt requests for help.

4. **"It's not acceptable to need help and not ask for it right away."** I like to explain it this way: "If you need help and ask for it, you may be afraid that we will be disappointed in you. So let's clear this up before our children arrive. If you tell us that you need help, we will take that as a sign that you, like us, really care about our children and care about doing your best possible job. We will *never* be disappointed in you for asking for help. Never. We will however, *guarantee* that we will be disappointed if you know you need help and don't let us know as soon as possible."

I also like to tell staff that the child's own parent doesn't try to raise the child by herself or himself. A parent may ask a spouse, their own parents, a neighbor, a best friend, or a professional for help. So there is absolutely no expectation that a child's staff person is supposed to figure everything out without assistance.

## Teaching Staff How Not to Ask for Help

We should take a few minutes during orientation to teach staff the professional and effective way to get assistance. First, we begin by giving them examples of how not to do it. Whining is at the top of the list. These statements are also not good:

- ☐ "I've tried everything!" (No one has ever tried everything.)

- ☐ "Nothing works! I give up!" (We don't give up until we can honestly say that we have used every possible resource available to us at camp.)

- ☐ "These kids are impossible! They'll never learn." (We get what we expect; if we give up on the ability of children to learn, then we lose and they lose.)

- ☐ "I can't do this!" (We want staff to say the same things that we want children to say when faced with difficult challenges: "I can't do this yet" and "I want to learn how to do this better" and "I need to figure out how to do this" and "This is hard; I can do hard things, especially if I get others to help me.")

You may want to add to the list other examples that you have heard in the past. I strongly recommend that these ineffective things be presented to staff in a memorable, creative way instead of just listing them in a manual or on the flipchart. One of the best ways is to go to some staff before this particular part of orientation and ask them to act out the examples in front of the whole group. Present a simple situation where staff might need help and then have the pre-selected staff show the ineffective approaches. This whole demonstration probably won't take more than two minutes at most. If they ham it up and whine a lot, then the rest of the staff will be entertained and pay more attention.

## How to Ask for Help: Three Effective Steps

Next, of course, we want to demonstrate exactly how we *do* want staff to ask for help. Have the staff who presented the ineffective examples help you show the following three steps:

1. **Tell the supervisor what is happening and explain what you want to happen instead.** ("The group keeps excluding this one camper. I really think it's cruel. She's

starting to hate camp. The problem is that I don't think she knows how to make friends and it's true that she tends to be kind of down and real negative. I don't know if this is because of how the other girls treat her or just the way she is. So I want to find some ways to teach her to fit in better but I also want the other kids in the group to stop dumping on her."

2.  **Tell what you've done so far and what has happened as a result.** This step is very important, yet it's the one that is most frequently left out by people who haven't been taught the right way to ask for help. It's the step that shows you're professional. You're not whining, not helpless, and not looking to be rescued. It shows that you've made a responsible effort to first work things out on your own. ("What I've tried so far is....")

3.  **Tell your supervisor that you'd appreciate getting some more ideas of what else you could try.** This says that you're looking for support and not trying to dump your job on someone else.

## How to Respond When Staff Ask for Help

Our basic approach here is to let staff know that they have made a good choice by asking for help. Staff may ask for help, however, in three different ways, and an expert supervisor will distinguish between them to respond most effectively.

### Situation One: the staff member asks for help, using the three-step technique that we outlined above.

☐ We affirm and praise their choice by saying something like, "Telling me about this and asking for help is smart." There's a reason that I use the specific word *smart*. Staff often feel weak or stupid when they ask for help; we are directly countering that apprehension by doing more than just saying that they've made the "right" choice. We say that it is smart. Smart people ask for help instead of keeping it to themselves. Smart means not only knowing what you know, but knowing what you *don't* know.

- ☐ Since they ask for help in exactly the right way, we want to specifically reinforce with a compliment by saying something like this: "You're telling me what's going on and what you've done about it. That's exactly the right way to ask for help; nice work...."

- ☐ Now we speak to them about the problem and provide guidance.

**Situation Two: The staff person asks for help, but in one of the ineffective ways that we described above. For example, she or he whines and says, "There's no point in trying; nothing will work; these kids are impossible...."**

- ☐ Again we affirm and praise their choice by telling them that asking for help is a *smart* thing to do.

- ☐ Then we just present a better way to ask so that they hear it in the correct form. We say, "OK, when we ask for help here's the best way to do it; first tell me what's going on and then tell me what you've tried so far...." Please note the use of the word "we" in "when we ask for help..." This is done to reduce any potential defensiveness by the staff person and show them that we are working through this together.

- ☐ Now we speak to them about the problem and provide guidance.

**Situation Three: The staff person asks for help, but does so later than she or he should.**

This is a very common supervision situation, so it's good to study how to respond.

- ☐ First, as I bet you've guessed, we're going to do exactly what we did before—affirm and praise the staff person's choice to ask for help by saying that it is smart.

- ☐ If they haven't asked for help in the best way, we can do what we did in Situation Two above.

- ☐ Now we speak to them about the problem and provide guidance.

- ☐ But we're going to finish differently by trying to teach them how to ask for help in a more timely way in the future. We do this by asking one of my favorite supervisor questions: *"How did you decide when to talk to me about this?"* Be sure to ask this calmly and without any critical edge to your voice.

☐  This is a terrific question because it makes staff think for themselves about when they should ask for help. Now please be prepared: some staff will respond with, "I know, I should have told you sooner...." We need to be sure that they really understand the importance of coming to us right away. So we can ask: "Why would that have been better?" Getting staff to think and talk about this is much more effective than lecturing them.

☐  We can also say, "It's really helpful to both of us when we talk about stuff like this as soon as it starts to happen. We want to be sure that we're getting the best possible support to you as fast as possible so you don't have to wait for it or hang out there on your own...."

☐  Focus on future choices by saying, "So if this sort of thing comes up again, what's your feeling about when it's best to let me know and talk about it?" Please notice this is a question; it's much more effective than concluding with an admonition like, "So next time, don't wait!"

☐  In summary, we want to teach without making staff defensive about their misjudgment and without losing sight of the fact that they did do the right thing, although not soon enough. Our focus is just on refining their skill so that they make even better choices next time.

## How to Respond When Staff Do Not Ask for Help

Sometimes staff don't ask for help because they don't know that they need it. But if they do know and don't ask, we can respond as follows:

☐  As in Situation Three above, we can explain in a positive way that asking for help is valued.

☐  The most important thing to do in this situation is to speak briefly with the staff person about their feelings and demonstrate that we understand them. We can ask, "Were you worried that if you told people about this, they might think that you weren't handling it well?" Regardless of how the staff person answers, we can affirm that having such feelings makes perfect sense. The issue, we explain, is how we *act* when we have these feelings.

☐ We can say: "Working at camp is hard. These are challenging things we are trying to do. When I first worked with kids I didn't want to ask for help, and I'll tell you why. It was important to me to make people feel like I knew what I was doing, and I thought that if I asked for help, they'd think I was in over my head. But now I know that if I ask for help in a way that shows that I'm working and not giving up, people will respect that."

☐ I also like to add: "What makes camp a team effort is that no one expects us to try to do a job this hard by ourselves...."

## Demonstrating Understanding

Staff always want to know that we understand how they feel, but this is especially important when they are feeling frustrated or facing special challenges.

Please memorize these three words: "I've been heard." That's our target. When people speak to us, especially about frustrations, fears, disagreements, or other strong emotions, we want to make them feel that they have been heard.

There are four ways to show staff that we've really heard them.

1.  **Tell them what you "got" from what they said.** In other words, state your understanding out loud. Just repeat it. Not word for word. Just give a summary so that they know you can state what they are feeling. Don't make this a "workshoppy" thing that sounds like pseudo-psychotherapy. Please don't preface it with what has become a cliché—"I hear you saying...." Just pretend that the message they sent is a ball; hold it up in the air to show that you received it. Try to do this before you throw your own message ball back.

If a staff person says, "It's like, I keep thinking I'm missing something because whatever I say, you know, this kid just acts like he doesn't have to listen to anything I say. He just turns away like I wasn't even talking."

If I'm the supervisor and I say, "Yeah, I understand..." or "Sure, I know what you're saying...," although this is a good start, I've only *said* that I understand. Please note that I haven't said what that understanding *is*. Trust is built when I *prove* understanding by stating it.

So it would be better if I said:

Me: "So it's like you're not even there."

Staff Person: "Exactly! (I've been heard.)"

Me: "And you're worried that maybe he ignores you because of the way you're talking to him, or what you're saying."

Staff Person: "Yeah. (I've been heard.) It's like, is it me? Am I missing something, or is he like this with everybody?"

2.  **We can say what we think they are feeling, even if they haven't expressed the feelings out loud.** To do this, we can ask a question that shows that we've tried to put ourselves in their emotional shoes.

    Staff Person: "She's still doing the same dumb stuff she did when she got here."

    Supervisor: "No change."

    Staff Person: "Zero."

    Supervisor: "So this is frustrating, like you're not getting anywhere?"

    Staff Person: "Yeah. (He understands how I feel.)"

3.  **Ask follow-up questions.** This is one of the best ways to show someone that we are listening and care about what they are saying. We can ask for an example, or when the last time was that the child acted in that way, or about how the other children are responding to the behavior—

anything that helps the staff person be more specific while showing that we are really hearing them.

4. **We can personalize our understanding of their feelings by relating our own experiences.** This proves that we've felt just like they have in similar circumstances. This is our moment to say, "This sounds like a kid I used to tutor in an after-school program..."

   Important fine point: only tell enough of your own story to establish that you have experience with this type of situation—that you've "been there." Do not go on for five or ten minutes talking about your past, because this may shift focus from further discussion of the staff member's immediate concerns. If describing how you handled the child from your past in a step-by-step manner will be useful, then save these additional details until after the staff person has fully disclosed her or his feelings and you're both ready to brainstorm about solutions.

## "Perfect" Doesn't Build Trust

I remember being a young counselor with a difficult child in my group. I'll call him "Biff." You know this child. Biff is the child who is both the irresistible force *and* the immovable object. I was reluctant to tell my supervisor that I was having problems because I was one of the youngest staff members the camp had hired that summer and I didn't want to give anyone extra reasons to believe that I couldn't handle my job.

I was playing a catching and throwing game with my group that my father had taught me when I was a boy. Each time you catch the ball, you take a step back before you throw it, thereby steadily increasing the distance of the throw. My supervisor, who I'll call Ted (but his name was really Tom....), was walking over at the exact moment that Biff caught the ball. Biff smirked (a Biff specialty), and then purposely threw the ball way over my head. He also made a remark that I can't remember anymore—but it was some disrespectful wise-guy thing. I *do* remember how embarrassed I was that Ted had seen this.

Ted was a gymnastics coach and physical education teacher at one of the local high schools. He looked the part—muscles layered neatly over more muscles. He seemed very nice, but we had not had any extended conversations. He was about twice my age and had been working with kids for as long as I had been alive.

So when Biff picked this moment for an extra display of Biffness, my stomach contracted to the size of the baseball that I was now chasing. Yes, I had thought of telling Biff that he had to go get the ball himself, but—I'm guessing you can finish this sentence yourself.

Ted approached and asked me how it was going and I lied and said "fine." There was no way I was going to tell him how nuts this kid was making me and how much anger I was feeling towards him.

Ted leaned toward me as if to whisper something. I saw it coming—the lecture on how I had to do a better job of controlling the kids in my group.

And then Ted did something very surprising that taught me one of the most important things I would use when I became a supervisor myself.

## Being Honest Builds Trust

He lowered his voice and said, "Is this kid *always* like this?" Before I could answer, he whispered, "Man, that's the kind of behavior stuff that can send us back to the drawing board...."

Well, I couldn't believe it. I didn't know what to say. Big, strong, experienced Ted was telling me that this little kid was getting to *him*?

He continued. "The kid has nice timing, too. Waits until the boss walks up." Ted smiled. "Obviously we're dealing with a pro here..."

So he *knew*! Ted understood how embarrassing this was.

At that moment, I felt like a ton of weight had dropped from my shoulders. New thoughts came flooding in. Maybe this isn't my fault. Maybe this kind of kid would be tough even on more experienced people. Maybe the anger and frustration I'm feeling isn't a sign that I don't know what I'm doing. Maybe it's just normal to feel this way. Maybe everyone would feel these things with a kid like Biff. Maybe I can learn how to do this better.

And more thoughts: My supervisor is an alright guy. He understands. He's been here. He can help me. He won't think I'm stupid if I tell him that sometimes I feel like losing this kid in the forest. Maybe he'll help me lose this kid in the forest....

So that day, and in the days that followed, Ted and I talked. We made some plans. Ted offered to spend some time with my group so that he could help me diagnose what was going on with Biff. I gratefully accepted his offer and watched him as he skillfully developed credibility not only with Biff but with my whole group. I noticed how he knelt down and got *quieter* when he was upset instead of trying to stand over them imperiously and lecture to them.

Years later, I went from being an insecure counselor to a somewhat secure counselor to an insecure supervisor. In an echo of my earlier days, I was now one of the youngest supervisors the camp had ever hired. I was worried that the staff would think that I didn't know how to do my job. I imagined them all silently asking, "Why did they make him a supervisor?" I pictured some of them adding, "...instead of me?"

So I made a mistake and tried to look perfect. When faced with challenging kids, my first instincts were to pretend that nothing gets to me. "I am the master of all challenging children!" Not only was this not true, it wasn't smart to pretend that it was true. And fortunately, in a few days, I remembered the lesson demonstrated by Ted's honesty. I realized that I had not trusted him when I thought he was perfect. *I only began trusting him when he made an effort to show me that he was not.*

## Positive Messages for Staff Who Are Having a Hard Time with Challenging Children

Challenging kids can wear anyone down. Part of our work on Path 3 is to recognize this and let staff know that they are good people who are trying to do a hard job.

Suppose we're talking with a staff person about a child or children with challenges. We want to praise and reinforce the staff person for "hanging in there" and for continuing to care. They may be feeling "down." They may be feeling weak, worried, insecure, or like a failure. We want to help them fight potential burnout by lifting their spirits and showing them how much we appreciate their efforts to try new approaches.

What follows is a "tool box" of messages that we can present to staff in these situations. We wouldn't say all of them to one person; these are just options from which we can pick what is most appropriate for the circumstances. Exact words are given for each message, but these are not intended as "scripts." We all have different styles of speaking and we may want to adapt how we say things depending on who is receiving the message.

1. What this child is doing (or not doing) is bothering you. That shows that you care about what happens to this camper. If you didn't care, it wouldn't bother you, right? You'd say, "The heck with it, it's not my fault, and it's not my problem."

2. The fact that you want to do something about this problem shows that you care about your entire group. You know that this is not just about one camper but how this camper is affecting the group. A lot of staff forget this....

3. This shows that you care about yourself. If you just worried about this situation but kept it all inside, that would wear you down....

4. Talking to me about this shows that you care about me. You know that I need to know what's going on to do my job and to support you. I appreciate that.

5. Your talking with me about this problem shows that you care about your job and about doing it well.

6. Talking to me about how we should handle this situation shows that you're not a conceited person—that you're not "stuck up" or a person who thinks they "know everything."

7. When you ask me for advice about this stuff, that says that you respect me and my experience.

8. The fact that you're bothered by what the campers are doing shows that you know what good behavior is. And that you've got high standards. Have you ever been to a mall or a playground and seen the kinds of behaviors that some

parents let their kids get away with? Sometimes the adults don't even pay attention or don't even see it. You see it. We see it. That's because we know that kids can do better.

9.    Your concern about this problem shows that you know why you're here. Kids like this are the ones that need us the most. These kids require harder work. But they are also the ones in which we can make the biggest differences.

10.   You're persistent. You don't quit because things are hard. You know, just about anyone can do this job if the campers do everything they're suppose to do and act perfectly all the time. What makes us different is that we keep at it even when it's hard. Let me ask you something: is it possible that other adults have seen this child and given up? That they've said there's no way to fix it, nothing more to try? I mean is it possible—we can't be sure, but is it possible—that we are the only ones who are still working to help this child?

11.   You're honest. You could have kept this to yourself. It's usually easier to keep stuff like this inside. A lot of times I don't want to show that I'm having problems because I don't want people to think I don't know what I'm doing.

12.   You're paying attention to one of the biggest things we talked about during orientation, which is that it's important to ask for and accept help and not try to do all of this by yourself.

13.   This shows that you know you're powerful. You know that if we keep at this we can make a difference for this child that might last for her/his whole life.

14.   You're still hanging in here with this camper. That shows that out of all the people in the world that we could have hired, you are exactly the kind of person we were looking for—a kind of person that is hard to find. It's not that you're perfect or that you know how to do everything. None of us are like that. We were looking for someone who cares, who doesn't quit, and who is always willing to keep learning and trying new things—someone we can work together with to help the kids who need it the most.

## Helping Staff Be Patient in Difficult Situations

I find it useful to ask staff to think about how long they believe it took for the behaviors, attitudes, or problems of a challenging child to develop. They will know that this did not happen overnight. We can then follow up by asking if it makes sense to believe that the solutions may require more than one step and take more than a few minutes, days, or weeks.

We can acknowledge out loud to staff that for some campers, the length of the entire camp session may not be enough to resolve a problem. If we can get it started and let children feel a positive difference, experience some success, and see for themselves that they can behave in better ways, then we can know that we did our best. We can hope that the children will continue to build on what they learned at camp and will make more progress outside of camp with the support of others.

An effective supervisor will help staff set realistic, specific, and limited goals that are achievable in the camp setting. We may not be able to make temper tantrums go away. But we *can* try to increase the number of times that a camper uses words to say that she or he is angry, instead of throwing things or calling other people names.

## My Favorite Question for Staff with Challenging Kids

This question helps staff work on a specific and realistic goal right away.

Ask, "What can we do to help this camper get some success in the next hour?"

We can work with staff on how to provide opportunities for this success. We can help them:

- ☐ identify some positive behaviors to look for and praise.

- ☐ think of a job, task, or responsibility that they can give to the child that is likely to be handled with success and can then be the subject of praise.

- ☐ identify one negative behavior that the child engages in (instead of trying to deal with all of them at one time) and pinpoint one specific, positive thing that we want the child to do in place of the negative behavior.

☐  teach and reinforce that one positive behavior during the next 60 minutes, not only with the problematic camper but with all the campers, so that everyone in the group serves as a good model for the others.

## The Biggest Secret for Supporting Staff Who Have Challenging Children

*We must make sure that our supervision of a staff person who is working on an ongoing, challenging situation does not primarily revolve around that negative situation. We do not want staff to believe that we will judge their performance at camp or define our relationship with them solely based on this challenge.*

This means that we must be sure to initiate contacts with the staff person about things that have nothing to do with the challenge. We need to visit their group and just play. We need to walk over and ask them about participating in the special event on Friday. We need to just make sure that every time we walk up to the staff person, she or he does not need to cringe and expect that we will always ask, "So what's going on with Biff?"

Sometimes we will speak to the staff person about the problem she or he is working on, but we don't need to do this every single time we interact. We will use our best judgment to achieve some balance between having encounters that relate to the challenge and having ones that do not.

If we *do* speak about Biff, we should be sure to also ask the staff person, "So how are the other campers doing?" If the staff person answers this in terms of how the campers are responding to Biff, we can discuss that. But be sure to have the staff person also talk about how the other children are doing in ways that have nothing to do with the challenging camper.

It's important that we do what we can to make sure that the staff person continues to focus on the entire group and doesn't get bogged down in problems posed by just one camper.

## Communicating with Our Director

Just as we taught staff to speak to their supervisors promptly about certain situations, we need to remember that it is part of our responsibility to *our* supervisor—the director or assistant director, for example—to let her or him know when a child or children are posing unusual challenges. This is particularly true when we believe that we may not be able to deal effectively with a challenge using our present resources at camp.

When we believe that one child or a few children are draining most of a staff person's energy and distracting her or him from serving the other campers in the group, we will work with the staff person on this situation. If the problem continues, then we will want to get our own supervisor involved in the problem-solving and decision-making process.

# Chapter Twelve

# Reverse Engineering

Staff feel supported when they have a positive, professional working relationship with their supervisor. Such a relationship can make them feel respected, appreciated, and motivated.

So how do we build such relationships at camp? Ironically, the correct place to begin is at . . . the end.

## The Reverse Engineering Process

The process of starting with the desired finish and working backwards to figure out how to get there is often called "reverse engineering." This process is frequently used by businesses. Suppose that we've decided to go into the business of manufacturing commercial dishwashing machines for camps. It would be a common approach for us to find other companies who make such machines, purchase the machines, and then take these finished products completely apart to study how they were made. As long as patents and other protected material are respected, this information could be used when we design our own machine.

We might take another approach. We could write a description of our "dream" machine and then work with designers to figure out what components we would need to produce such a finished product.

Both of these approaches start at the end. We look at a finished result and work backwards to identify how we can produce that result.

## Using Reverse Engineering as Supervisors

I experimented some years ago to see if the reverse engineering process would work with intangible things like relationships. I was pleased to discover that this process is a very fast and efficient way to help people identify specific skills that can be used to produce successful professional relationships. I developed a two-question method to guide people through this process. I will describe it here so that you can try it for yourself right away.

**Question One:     What positive things do you want the staff that you are supervising to say about you when this camp season is over?**

You can vary this question by changing the time period. You can add: after the first time they meet you, after orientation is concluded, at the end of the first day or week of camp, and so on.

You can also ask this question about other relationships. For example, you can ask what positive things you want to be said about you by your boss, by other supervisors, by campers, or their parents.

**Question Two:     Since people are going to talk about me behind my back, what can I do to increase the probability that what they say will match the positive things I listed in my answer to Question One?**

## Practicing with Question One

You didn't think that I was going to ask you to read this without practicing, did you? Of course not. And as an incentive to get you to try this right now, while operators are standing by, I'll throw in today—and today only—an offer *not available in any other book*!

That's right! If you act *right now*, you'll also get my special secret technique that makes answering Question Two a breeze!

But wait—there's *more!* As a super extra book bonus, you'll get over 175 specific examples of things you can do or say that will help build strong relationships with the people you supervise!

So why delay? *Try it now!* It's as easy as picking up your pen! Here's all you have to do....

Start by answering Question One. Get some paper and take about three minutes to make a list of what positive things you want staff to believe about you. What qualities and characteristics do you want them to say you have?

In responding to this question, it's sometimes helpful to try to list things that would finish this statement:

"My staff supervisor is someone who is _____."

We could list, for example: flexible, open-minded, creative, and so on.

But I have one request that will help make this brief activity more valuable to you. *Please write down only those words that you believe staff don't already say about you.* Let me explain what I mean. If you think that just about every person you've worked with before has believed that you are a world-class listener, then don't bother to put "listener" on your list. Instead, stretch yourself and write down words that you *don't* believe people generally conclude about you—but you wish that they *did.* In other words, this should be a kind of "goal list" for you.

Please remember that there are no correct answers to this. Write down whatever is important to you. Thanks!

## The Power of Writing

Before we move on to Question Two, I'd like to tell you about something interesting that happens in workshops when I ask people to take a few minutes to respond to the first question. When they are done, I ask: "How many of you have made a list like this, in writing, anytime in the last 6 months?" The first time I asked this question, I had no idea what to expect. I was stunned when only two people in the rather large meeting room raised their hands. So I extended the time to a year. Then two years. I think at most two more hands went up.

I've asked this question for quite a few years now, in large and small groups, and the percentage of people who have made such a written list is very, very small.

I always follow up with this question: "How many of you would agree that if we did have such a written list of what we want people to believe about us in our professional relationships, we would be much more likely to act in ways that make people see that we have these qualities?" Now every person puts a hand in the air.

## Practicing with Question Two

Now comes the best part—Question Two. What are some specific things that we can do or say that will lead people to believe that we have the qualities we wrote about in response to Question One? Before working on this, let's be clear that we are not talking about creating "false images" to make people believe things about us that aren't really true. When we do or say things that creative people do or say, for example, then staff will believe we are creative because, in fact, we *are* acting creatively.

Before you work on this second question, here, as promised, is the trick to making this much easier. Ask the "Who do I know?" question. Pick one item on your Question One list at random— for example, "creative"—and ask yourself, "Who do I know that I or other people already say is creative?" These people don't have to be camp people, of course.

When you've thought of such a person or people, all you have to do now is ask, "What do these people do or say that makes us believe they are so creative?"

Check your responses to be sure that they are specific things that you could see or hear. If a response seems too general, just remember to ask, "But what are people seeing or hearing that makes them conclude that this is true?"

So in summary, you just ask: "Who do I know?" and "What do they do or say?"

Why does this approach make this process simpler? Because when we actually picture a real person, it gives us some specific behavior to study instead of trying to abstractly figure out what things we should do ourselves.

Please note: on occasion people ask me what they should do if they cannot think of a person who is already labeled, for example, a great listener or a really flexible person? This is OK. While it is very important to have mental pictures of people with these qualities, there's no rule that says we have to know who they all are right this minute. We should make it a personal goal to search for such people because *studying what they do and say is one of the fastest ways to improve our skills as supervisors.*

Time to practice. Please pick three words from your list. For each word, ask: "Who do I know that I or other people already use this word to describe?" and "What does this person do or say that makes people believe the word is true?" As always—please do your best to be specific.

Thanks for working on Question Two. Our goal, of course, is to keep working on this question throughout our life to learn as much as possible from the successful choices of those around us.

## Look in the Liver

The Liver at the end of the book has a section of almost 200 reverse engineered skills that we can use every day to build strong relationships with others.

## Chapter Thirteen

# Manage Undesired Staff Behavior In Positive Ways

Sometimes staff do not do what we want them to do. They may make a mistake (yell at campers as an ineffective form of discipline) or simply not work to their full potential (idly sit on the grass instead of actively playing a game with their groups). In this book, we'll refer to this as undesired behavior.

We have two goals on Path 4. First, we want to teach staff how to replace undesired behavior with better choices. Second, we want to teach staff stronger decision-making and problem-solving skills so they can make good choices on their own.

## A Boss Is Not "Bossy"

The most frequent mistake that camp supervisors make in handling undesired staff behavior is to ignore it until it gets "really bad." This greatly undermines a supervisor's credibility, which can be almost as dangerous as swimming without a buddy.

It's easy to understand how this happens. Supervisors don't want to seem like harsh taskmasters. In the informal world of camp, supervisors want to be "liked" and to be treated by staff as a friend. Many supervisors, therefore, don't want to be viewed as a "boss."

Here's the deal: *If we are a camp supervisor, we are a boss.* Even if we're at a not-for-profit camp where we are supervising volunteers, we're still a boss. This means that our job on Path 4 is to ensure that people do what they are expected to do, to the best of their abilities. If they don't, then it is our job to teach staff to make better choices right away.

## Positive Images

I know that "boss" has a negative connotation to many people. From time to time I've worked for bosses that have helped create this negative image. But I've also worked for some bosses that have been fantastic. They were kind, warm, nice, honest, and caring. They were terrific mentors.

I think that a lot of the perception problem arises when we confuse the word "boss" with "bossy." Please know that we can enforce high standards and make sure that staff are doing their best possible work without being "bossy." We do this by being respectful and skilled in how we communicate with staff.

So the key here is to not fight the fact that we're a boss, but to focus instead on asking ourselves what *kind* of a boss we want to be.

An excellent boss is a teacher, a coach, and a leader. All of these things are positive, not negative.

## The "Nice" Problem

A supervisor can be friendly and fun. Being an excellent supervisor doesn't mean that we stop being nice. But there are times when our upholding of high performance standards requires us to be firm and to direct others to refine their skills. Sometimes we have to tell people to do things they might not want to do. In these moments, "nice" means always being respectful, considerate, polite, and not seeking to embarrass. It can also include being understanding and forgiving of mistakes, especially if the person who has made the mistakes shows regret and a determination to learn how to correct them.

Good parents and teachers know that being nice doesn't mean they say "yes" to a child when their responsibilities require them to say "no." Sometimes their decisions will make children unhappy, but if their relationships with the children are built on respect, then the relationships can survive such moments. The same is true for camp supervisors.

We can make an interesting parallel here. You know how campers who become junior counselors or counselors-in-training often have a problem making the transition from being a camper to being a leader? We tell these young people that they aren't campers anymore and that they must accept that their relationships with the other kids may change because, as junior leaders, they have different and greater responsibilities.

The same thing is true when we become a supervisor.

## Supervising Friends

But what if we're supervising people who may be close friends? *People who are really our friends will not act in ways that embarrass us or put us in compromising positions.* And sometimes we must take our friends aside, look them right in the eye, and tell them that.

If a staff person who is a friend tells you to look the other way about some undesired behavior or gives you a hassle for doing your job, you can say something like this: "*Because* you're my friend, you know how important it is to me to do a really good job as a supervisor here, and you'll help me not mess it up."

If the friend persists in acting in a way that puts you in a difficult position, and isn't willing to talk about finding a reasonable solution to the problem, then you'll probably be having an even more serious conversation with this person about what kinds of things you need in a friend.

## Credibility: The Law of Extrapolation

*A supervisor's credibility comes from making consistent responses to staff behavior.*

Certain staff join a frequent sitter program in which they sit under trees while their campers play games or do other activities. If a supervisor walks by and doesn't speak to staff about this repeated behavior, staff are going to conclude that they don't have to work very hard. No consequence—therefore no credibility.

Suppose we tell staff that during parts of the day that are governed by a specific schedule, they must follow that schedule and not disregard it unless they speak with us first. When we see staff who are "off schedule," we must respond to this immediately and effectively. There are two reasons for this.

The first reason is obvious. If staff are in the wrong place with their campers and we walk by and don't say anything, then it's reasonable for staff to conclude that they don't have to follow this rule.

But the second reason we must respond promptly to undesired behavior is more subtle. If a staff person doesn't follow the schedule and we don't say or do anything about it, the problem is not just that people won't believe us about staying on the schedule. Staff will begin to extrapolate—that is, they will infer that if we don't have to be believed about the *schedule* rule, then maybe we don't have to be believed about *other* rules, either.

I call this the *Law of Extrapolation*: If we ignore undesired behavior, and a staff person extrapolates, our credibility evaporates.

And wait—it gets worse. Suppose one staff person, Bill, is following the schedule but sees that we don't do anything when Roger *doesn't* follow the schedule. What does Bill now infer about our credibility?

To secure our credibility, we must have a conversation with ourselves, preferably before staff arrive. We must decide whether we really *are* serious about enforcing rules and maintaining high performance standards. Either we are or we aren't. If we aren't, or we're not sure, I can tell you one thing with complete confidence: staff can smell this. And many will take advantage of it, just like campers testing a counselor who is uncertain about what behavior is allowable.

## So What Do We Say When We See Undesired Behavior?

OK, so suppose we're now re-motivated to take action when staff engage in undesired conduct. What exactly do we do? There are two parts to our response to undesired behavior.

| Part One: | We respectfully but firmly tell them that what they are doing (or not doing) is not OK and we explain why. |
|---|---|
| Part Two: | We respectfully but firmly tell them, and if necessary teach them, what we want them to do instead. |

## Part One: Communicating That It's Not OK

The exact words that we use in Part One will be affected by our style of speaking, to whom we are speaking, whether this has happened with this staff person before, and other variables. Whatever words we choose, our most important guideline is to be respectful. We do not raise our voice or act "bossy." We do not embarrass the staff person. When possible, we speak to the person privately, not in front of their campers or other staff.

In our situation with the staff person who is not following the schedule, we might say: "Paul, your group is supposed to be at archery right now." Paul may then reply, "I know, but we got out of crafts five minutes late. I figured by the time we got there we wouldn't have time to make it worthwhile. And my guys don't really like archery anyway."

"Paul," we reply, "the problem here is that someone needs to know where your group is all of the time. If we need to speak with one of your campers or with you right away, we're going to look at the schedule and go to where you're supposed to be. If you're not there, it's not OK."

## Part Two: Telling & Teaching Staff What to Do Instead

Let's review. In Part One, we tell the staff person that they've made an incorrect choice. We explain why it's not correct. But our work is not done. Part Two is the part that is frequently left out— but it's essential.

The purpose of Part Two is to apply what I believe is the most important principle in working with undesired behavior, whether working with adults or children. I call this the *Law of Replacement*: "It is not enough to tell people to stop doing something wrong. We must also tell them immediately and specifically what we want them to do instead." In Part Two, our focus is positive: we are teaching the staff person what they are *supposed* to do in this kind of situation.

We might say something like this to Paul: "The deal here is that you just have to talk to me first. If you decide that you don't want to go to an activity because your kids don't like it, then please come to talk to me and I'll work with you and your group to see how to handle it. If you're running late and you don't feel there's enough time to get to your next activity, then please get a message to me or to the office that lets us know where you are going to be."

This approach is respectful. We didn't say to Paul, "Look, I don't care what happened at crafts or whether your guys are into this Robin Hood stuff or not. The schedule is the schedule. It's not complicated. You just follow it. End of story."

Instead, we demonstrated that we heard the problems Paul spoke about, and we explained to Paul what to do when he has those problems.

## A Preview of Advanced Technique: Teaching Problem-Solving

In our example above, we *told* Paul exactly what he was doing incorrectly, why it was incorrect, and what he should do when this situation arises again. This is the simplest, quickest, and most direct way to manage undesired staff behavior. It works fine. But there is another way we could do this. Instead of just telling Paul what we want him to know and do, we can try to get him to figure this stuff out for himself. We can invite him to talk with us about the problem and ask him some questions that will help him *discover* what was wrong with his choice and what he should do instead.

This approach is a little more challenging for us and for staff. But it yields greater benefits because it teaches staff how to make better decisions on their own. I will describe exactly how to do this more advanced approach in the next chapter.

## Please Dog-Ear This Page

Please grab your highlighter: This paragraph states one of the most important secrets for successful management of undesired behavior: *After correcting staff for handling something in an inappropriate way, we should be on a special lookout for them doing it correctly the next time, so that we can praise this better behavior.*

In our situation with Paul, we told him to stay on his schedule and talk to us first before changing it. If Paul comes to us later to speak to us about a schedule matter—whether it's about changing it, or his kids not liking something, or any other problem with it—we pounce on this event as an opportunity to say, "Paul, I'm glad you're talking to me about schedule stuff. You're coming to me first, which is exactly what we need you to do...."

## What Do We Do If Staff Don't Listen & They Keep Repeating the Same Undesired Behavior?

Electric shock.

## No, Come On—What Do We Do with These People?

No easy solutions here. Our main job at this point is to try to figure out which of three categories best applies to this staff person and respond to them accordingly.

## Category One Staff

A "Category One" person is someone who just doesn't "get it" yet, but seems willing to keep trying. Since, despite our efforts, the undesired behavior has not been corrected, we can go to our own supervisor—a director or assistant director, for example—and ask her or him for help using the same method that we taught to staff (Chapter Eleven). First, we describe the problem. Second, we tell what we've done so far to solve it. Third, we ask for more ideas. Sometimes it will be decided that you—if you haven't done so already—should spend an entire day with the staff person to observe how she or he responds to your coaching and modeling. The director may also want to observe the staff person. Sometimes it may be decided that it's best to switch the staff person's responsibilities or assignment.

And sometimes, you and the director will reluctantly decide that if (a) camp resources aren't reasonably available to bring the performance level of a staff person to an acceptable level, and (b) if the nature of the infractions or repeatedly poor performance are of a serious enough nature, then it's time to consider whether the person should remain on the staff.

## Category Two Staff

A "Category Two" situation is much easier, because here the staff person is someone who provides little or no evidence of caring or wanting to improve. You'll communicate this to your supervisor right away.

## Category Three Staff

Staff in this third category do something of a very serious nature that is on the "hot" list. Camps have policies for infractions of this type. Please be sure you are familiar with them.

## Techniques for Determining If Staff "Get It"

We can't really tell if staff understand what they are supposed to be doing if we just ask them, "Do you get what I'm saying?" Instead, I've learned to ask open questions—ones that don't give clues as to the appropriate answers. These questions help us to evaluate whether a person cares enough to keep working with us on raising their level of skill.

Let's start with one of my favorite questions:

"I want to be sure that I've done a good job explaining what needs to happen—what you need to do. Would you tell me what you believe it is, *so I know that I've explained it clearly*?"

Posing the question in this form is respectful. You've heard an adult shouting at a child (or a spouse): "Are you listening to me? What did I say?" That embarrassing confrontation is what we're trying to avoid here. By saying that we want to check to be sure that we did a good job communicating (which we do), we get the staff person to say out loud what she or he is supposed to do.

If a staff person has been repeatedly told to act differently but has not done so, we can ask them this:

"I've asked you to do X a few times now, but you're still not doing it. I need to learn more from you why that's happening. Would you please tell me?"

This question is very respectful and it gets the staff person to talk. If the staff person doesn't seem to care, then they have just catapulted themselves headfirst in the direction of Category Two. But sometimes, after ignoring what we've asked several times, staff will say something like, "Well I guess I just don't think it's important to do...." In this case we can try to teach them what a responsible person is supposed to do in this situation. We can say, "I'm glad you're telling me how you feel about this. I really need you to tell me things like this *earlier,* though. You told me that you were going to do it (the correct behavior), but you didn't. When you and I tell each other that we're going to do something, we need to be able to trust that we'll both do our best to do it—no exceptions. So if you don't think something is a good idea, it's your job to tell me that right away so that we can talk about it."

We then listen to their views, but *if what we're asking them to do is a requirement and not negotiable, we will explain why and stick to it firmly.* If they fail again to do what we are expecting, this is pretty clear evidence of Category Two behavior.

## An Obvious but Important Caution

I love it when people say "It goes without saying...." and then say it anyway. So here I go: It goes without saying that there are certain undesired behaviors that we cannot let staff repeat. If, for example, we believe that a counselor is not safely supervising campers, or is yelling in anger at campers without exercising self-control, then we may need to place someone else with their group right away until the problem is resolved.

## A Favorite Question to Wake Up Staff

A creative and attention-getting way to get staff to realize that a matter is serious is to ask this powerful question:

"So please tell me what I'm supposed to do now. (They'll look at you blankly, not understanding.) I've asked you to do X and you said that you'd do it. But you didn't. Twice. So what's my next move here?"

This question really helps staff understand that they have done something serious, because you're asking them to put themselves in your supervisory footwear. Getting staff to look at their behavior from your point of view will sometimes help them understand how their conduct affects others and that it can have a serious impact on our evaluation of their job performance.

Please know that in most cases, staff will shrug or say "I don't know" in response to this question. That's OK. We can respond as follows, using a respectful, calm tone, and not a threatening one. We say, "I need to go think about this. Would you please do the same and come back to me in about ten minutes and tell me what you're going to do differently to solve this problem? Thank you...." Then you walk away. This is very strong. How staff respond ten minutes later will tell you whether they are remorseful and trying to get themselves together, or disrespectful and believing that they can ignore you without consequences.

## Getting Our Boss Directly Involved

One way to let staff know that we are serious about their undesired behavior is to have them speak to our boss. Depending on the nature of the behavior, this is not something we typically choose to do right away, and before we do this we will want to speak to our director to be sure that she or he agrees that this is the appropriate next step.

When we do refer someone to our boss, we want to maintain respect. We also need to remember that if the staff person corrects the problem, we'll still be their supervisor and will work with this person every day. We can say: "You and I haven't solved this. I've explained this to the director and we both agree this has to be fixed right away. I think that we need to get someone else's ideas involved at this point and she/he would like to talk to you about this....."

## We're Defined by the Hard Things We Do, Not the Easy Ones

Working with staff on undesirable conduct is not an easy part of our job. The techniques reviewed in this chapter help us to do this work in a positive way while maintaining respectful relationships.

Everyone makes mistakes, and everyone can find ways to improve their skills. Sometimes staff need our guidance to make the best possible choices. We tell staff that the children with challenges may be the ones who need us the most. Similarly, coaching staff who need extra help to reach higher levels of performance is one of the most important Paths that we walk as supervisors.

## Coming Up....

As promised, the next chapter explains some advanced techniques to teach staff to develop sound, independent judgment.

And then, since *how* we say things to staff is as important as what we say, we'll review in Chapter Sixteen some specific phrases that show staff that we value ongoing improvement in ourselves and others.

# Chapter Fourteen

# Using Questions to Teach Problem-Solving & Decision-Making

The best supervisors act as effective teachers. One of the most important characteristics of effective teachers is that they don't try to "pour" knowledge into the passive heads of students. Instead, they develop more independent thinkers by using questions to guide students to actively *discover* the answers themselves. When we do this with staff, it deepens learning and it shows staff how to use good questions to solve problems on their own.

## Using Questions When Talking About Staff Undesired Behavior

In the last chapter, we explained a two-part method of communicating with staff about their undesired behavior. In Part One, we want staff to see that the choice they made was not correct; in Part Two, we want them to learn what to do instead.

In this chapter, we'll apply a more advanced approach to the method and use questions to help staff think more deeply about their behavior and how to make it better.

**Part One Questions**

In Part One, instead of saying "This is not OK to do," we can help staff to understand their choices by asking these questions:

- ☐   When X happened, what did you do? What choice did you make?

- ☐   What happened when you did that? Did it work? What was good about it? What was not good about it?

- ☐   What is the camp policy or procedure that we're supposed to follow in these situations? Did you follow it? Why not? What are we supposed to do if we've been told to do something, but we don't want to do it?

**Part Two Questions**

In Part Two, instead of saying, "This is what you are supposed to do....," again we can use good questions to lead staff to figure this out for themselves. Please remember: When staff participate in the problem-solving process, it gives them a greater "investment" in the solution. This increases their personal interest in making sure that a situation is handled better the next time. These are helpful questions to guide staff in thinking about appropriate replacement behavior:

- ☐   When X happened, what other options did you have?

- ☐   What could you have done differently, knowing what you know now?

- ☐   If this happened again, what would you do?

- ☐   Why would that be better than what was done before?

Please pay particular attention to that last question. It's the one I use to make sure that staff really understand how to improve their performance. If staff cannot answer the question with confidence, then I know that more teaching will be required.

## An Example of Using Questions to Teach Better Choices to Staff

If a counselor yells at children, we could do Part One by telling them that yelling isn't allowed and explaining why it doesn't work.

For Part Two, we could describe ways to bring the tension down and have calmer and more confident communication.

But as we've said, the best *teaching* here would more actively involve the counselor.

So let's listen in on a supervisor using questions to teach better choices:

## Part One: Communicate That the Choice Was Not OK

"Claire, the girls were really getting out of hand there for a few minutes. Would you talk to me about what they did and what you did?"

"Well they were just totally off the wall. I don't know what gets into them sometimes. They think they're so cool and grown up and then they act like babies."

"What were they saying to you?"

"They were calling me names and saying that all the stuff we were doing was stupid and that they hate me. Where do they get off talking like that? It's their fault; they never want to do anything."

"What did you do when they yelled at you?"

"I yelled back at them. I called them a bunch of babies. I know I'm not supposed to do that. I just lost it."

"Why aren't you supposed to do that?"

"Yell at them? Well, because then I'm just doing what they're doing, but I'll tell you, I don't know what to do with them sometimes."

"They can drive us crazy sometimes."

"Really."

"Well let's look at what you did, let's figure out if it worked, and let's look at other things we can do, OK?"

"Well it didn't work. They just got louder."

"When you yelled back, they just had to do it even bigger, so they'd be louder than you."

"Yeah."

"When you call them babies, what happens?"

(Claire seems to be thinking about it; she doesn't answer.)

"Do their defenses go up or down?"

"Up."

"Does that make it easier for them to listen to you or harder?"

"Harder."

"Sure. Good. So when we yell back at them, we're trying to show that we're in control, that we're the boss. Does it work? What do you think it looks like to the kids?"

"Definitely not in control."

"And what do we *want* to look like to them?"

"In control. Calm. Except I wasn't."

## Part Two: What the Staff Person Should Do Instead

"OK. So what could you do to show them that you are angry, but still in control?"

"I'm not sure."

"That's OK. Just think about it for a minute."

"I could tell them?"

"What could you say?"

"I'd say that I didn't want them to talk to me like that. I hate it when people scream at me. That I don't like to be blamed for their not having fun, because I don't think that's my fault."

"Great. How would you say it? Talk to me about the volume."

"Yeah, I know—I'd have to not shout."

"Sure. Now what else could we do to bring the tension down here. What about the way we're looking, or standing?"

"I don't know what you mean."

"OK. You know the moment when you really started to feel like you were losing it? What if you sat down right at their feet and started telling them how you were feeling? What do you think would happen?"

(She laughs.) "I think they'd kick me."

"True, you'd be an easier target...."

"I think that if I sat down, it might calm things down, and we could talk about stuff. Maybe they'd cool off a little. It might help me get a grip, too. But I'd really want to tell them I'm mad."

"And you can. What we're talking about is *how* to talk about our feelings. And you're exactly right about what happens—when people sit, the tension goes down. And then you can hold a meeting with everyone. Who should do most of the talking?"

"Them."

"Right. And what would this talk be about?"

"Well, why they weren't having fun and what we could do

about it. And I could tell them that it's not any fun for me to listen to them crabbing all of the time."

"And what would we say to them if they started shouting again?"

"I'd tell them that we don't want to listen to shouting. I'm not going to shout, and they're not going to shout. They can tell me how they feel, but they've got to talk just regular—just say it."

"Great. And if everyone told how they felt, and everyone listened, what do you think would happen to the odds of this problem getting better?

"Better odds, yeah."

### More Part Two: Making Sure That the Staff Person Understands What Choices to Make Next Time This Happens

"OK, so let's make sure we've got it. It's tomorrow morning and they start yelling again. We've had time to think now about how to best handle this. What are you going to do?"

"I'm going to sit down right away. I'm going to talk quietly and tell them that I'm mad too, but that we're going to talk about it. And listen to each other."

"That's it. You've got it. You did a great job thinking this through. Now if this happens again, you can be confident that you've got a good way to handle it. I'll tell you, having these sit-down meetings with campers can be hard, because they're letting their emotions out. If you feel like you want help with that—if you think it would be helpful for me to be there when your group talks this through, please let me know. I'd be happy to do that, but you decide and let me know."

## Building Better Brains: Get Staff to Talk First

The supervisor in the above example used my favorite tool to get staff to think about their choices. It's really simple. Just say, "*Please talk to me about X* (the situation)...." Use this tool to get staff to think and speak about the problem or issue *first,* before we start analyzing it for them. This gives them more responsibility and makes them think harder.

## Using Open Questions and "We"

Please also note two other things in the supervisor's conversation with Claire. The supervisor asked a lot of open questions. When Claire wasn't sure how to respond, the supervisor asked narrower, easier questions to help Claire have success. The supervisor also used the word "we" a lot. "How could *we* handle this?" "What would *we* say?" This helps the staff person see this as a team effort and also says that this is not just her or his problem—it's a common problem that we all face and all have to be prepared to handle well. Using "we" also helps staff feel less defensive when speaking about their mistakes.

## Using Questions to Help Staff Decide What to Do

I was in the office of Larry Bell, a director of an outstanding day camp in Markham, Ontario. It was orientation week at Camp Robin Hood, and I was sitting in a corner chair making some notes when a young group counsellor walked in. (She was a Canadian staff person, so she gets two "l's.") She said to Larry, "I don't know if you remember, but I have my sister's wedding to go to this weekend and there's all this stuff I need to do for it, and things I'm supposed to be at. I was wondering, would it be OK if I had my junior counsellor make half of the parent calls?"

At Camp Robin Hood, group counsellors are supposed to call and introduce themselves to the campers and their parents before the first session begins.

Larry was leaning against his desk. He smiled and asked, "Well, let's think about that for a moment. What are your thoughts about it?"

She looked ready for this. "Well," she said, "I know that it's important to speak to all of the families, but I was thinking that it's important for the junior counsellor to get introduced, too, so if she did some and I did some, it would be OK. And then of course I could call the ones I didn't talk to the first week of camp, when the wedding is over."

Larry said, "So you think that one of the advantages to this is that it would give both of you a chance to speak to the families?"

"Right!" she said brightly.

"OK," continued Larry, "Let's keep going. Are there any other positives to it?"

"It would save time. I mean ordinarily it wouldn't be so important, but this week is just so crazy."

"It *would* save you time. Can you think of anything else that's on the positive side?"

She shook her head no. Larry asked, "OK, then let's ask what the negatives might be. Can you think of any?"

The counsellor thought for a moment. "Well, I know the other counsellors will be making all the calls themselves, so this would be an exception. But I'd call all the other families next week...."

"OK, anything else?"

"I can't think of any."

"Well let's keep thinking about this together. How do you think the parents might feel about this if, before camp starts, they hear from the junior counsellor instead of you?"

"They might wonder why the counsellor didn't call, I suppose. But the j.c. could explain."

"Yes. And how do you think the parents might feel if the actual counsellor didn't call?"

At this point the counsellor's face showed that she was figuring out where this was going. She began to back out of the room and said, "You know, if you don't think it's a good idea, I'll just make the calls. I'll find time to do it. You're right. I should make the calls."

But Larry wasn't just interested in the young lady reaching the right answer. He was interested in making sure that she knew what all of the right *questions* were, so that she would be able to ask them on her own in the future when making other decisions affecting camp families. So he smiled again and said, "That's OK, please stay a minute. Let's think it all the way through before we decide. What do you think some of the campers might feel if they didn't get to talk to the counsellor?"

"Well, I don't know. I think they'd be excited to talk to the junior counsellor." She stood there waiting for Larry to keep talking, but he didn't. He gave her time to think. And she did. She said that having the j.c. call wouldn't really help her, the counsellor, start up a relationship with the campers.

Larry said, "So we've looked at the positive things and the negative things. Where do you think we come out then?"

"I guess it's important that I get to all of the calls before camp starts. I will. I'll get it done."

Larry: "It sounds like you've made a good decision. I know this will be hard for you to get done, but I really appreciate that you'll do it personally. I'm sure the families will appreciate it, too. Thanks!"

## Post-Game Analysis...

When the counsellor walked into his office and made her request, Larry could have just said right away, "No, it's important that you make the calls yourself." Instead, he chose to use this as an opportunity to model and teach good decision-making. The staff person practiced asking these key questions: "What are the positive sides to this course of action?" and "What are the negative sides to this course of action?" To you and me, this may seem elementary, but there are a lot of young people (and I suppose older people, too) who have never been taught how to ask these questions.

In addition, the counsellor learned to ask another critical question: "How will this course of action affect all of the people involved?" And the follow-up: "What might people conclude if I do it this way?"

Notice how Larry ended the conversation. He told the counsellor that *she* had made a good decision. Making people more confident about their skills is an important part of teaching them to use them.

## Common Questions About Questions

What happens if the staff person doesn't come to the conclusion that we think they should? First, in the Liver of this book, there are many examples of questions that can be used to guide staff to rethink their conclusions and get back on track. Second, if staff don't figure out where we were trying to guide them, we just do what good teachers do. We describe the way we view things and explain what staff may have missed in their thinking.

Then staff will acquire a deeper understanding of why we believe another course of action is better, even if they don't agree. And most importantly, they will have seen the thoughtful, not arbitrary, process by which we arrived at the result.

## Time Out

Who's got time for this? Doesn't asking questions take a lot more time? Of course—lectures are always faster, and all good coaches and teachers will tell us that maximizing learning is more involved and more challenging than just telling people what we want them to do. Suppose Larry had been in the middle of five complicated things when the counsellor had entered his office, or the situation had required the staff person to do something immediately. In that case, he could have simply told her what he wanted her to do and then explained it another time.

Please remember that we do not have to use every situation as opportunities for teaching problem-solving and decision-making. When we can take extra moments to use more questions, the benefits are well worth the invested time.

## Being Prepared: Some Questions About Questions

What if staff say, "Just tell me what to do!" We can respond by saying that if we did, we would be doing only half our job. One half, we explain, is getting this problem solved. But the other half is for us to help the staff person feel confident so that when other problems like this come up, she or he will better know the steps to take and how to think it through.

What if staff respond to that by saying something like, "But you're in charge!" or "You're the boss!" We can say, "Right, and I want to be a good one. A good one is like a good coach—she/he helps people know that they are smart, and that if they go through the right steps, they will come up with good solutions."

What if the staff person responds to questions by saying "I don't know"? We can let them know that it's OK not to know. We can then ask, "How can we find out?" If the staff person doesn't know that either, we can tell her or him that we'll help. The key here is that we don't want people to think that they can make their responsibilities go away just by saying "I don't know." The lesson to teach staff is that it is OK not to know, but that "I don't know" is not the end—it's just a *beginning*.

## Questions vs. Statements

So how do we figure out when to ask questions instead of just giving our own opinions? We've already pointed out that not all situations call for teaching thinking skills, and sometimes time and other pressures don't give us the opportunity to teach in certain situations even if we wanted to. What we're looking for is a *balance*.

The best supervisors are very aware of when they are making statements and when they are asking questions. Please get in the habit of separating what you say into one of those two categories. Set two specific goals for yourself: First, try to have a greater number of questions than statements. Second, decide consciously which tool you are going to use. In other words, ask yourself, "Should I do this with statements or should I use questions?"

## How Do I Learn What Questions to Ask in Other Situations?

I've collected in the Liver of this book some great questions that I like to ask staff. I hope that you will review them and find them a helpful resource. These questions help us lead staff to:

☐    define problems

☐    identify potential options

☐    consider and evaluate options

☐    make sure that they have been comprehensive in their thinking

☐    look at things from the perspective of others

☐    get started solving problems and evaluating progress

☐    set deadlines and get assistance

☐    make the best use of available resources

☐    handle their own resistance or negativism

Now: any questions? I hope not. I hate questions....

# Chapter Fifteen

# Smoothies

The David & Dad fruit smoothie is made with the following ingredients:

- 2 cups of vanilla yogurt
- 2 cups of canned pineapple juice
- 2 cups of strawberries
- 2 bananas
- 4 to 6 ice cubes

You may add or substitute other types of fruit if you like.

Mix the ingredients in a blender and refrigerate them until chilled. Garnish individual glasses with a lemon slice or strawberry.

Serves four.

# Chapter Sixteen

# Tools for Tact

We can facilitate positive changes in others by creating an environment at camp that clearly values ongoing improvement. Getting staff to improve their skills and learn to make better choices is easier when staff see that we are doing the same thing. The following are some things that we want staff to hear us say. These "facilitating phrases" demonstrate to staff that we, as supervisors, are learning all of the time, just like we want staff to do.

- ☐ "I used to believe XYZ. Now I've come to believe ABC...."
- ☐ "I'm always trying to find better ways for me to do things."
- ☐ "I've got to find a better way to do this."
- ☐ "I've been trying to figure this out for years; I keep trying different things, and I've got it down better now, but I'm still working on it."
- ☐ "Something I keep working on is...."
- ☐ "I used to do this a different way. This new way is much better."

- ☐ "When I did it this way, I didn't like how it worked. Then I started trying to do ABC, and that was so much better."

- ☐ "When I first started working with kids, I thought that I was supposed to XYZ. Then I watched some other people that had more experience and I learned that ABC is the way to go."

- ☐ "One of the changes I've made is...."

- ☐ "One of the things that I do differently now is...."

- ☐ "I wish I had known this a long time ago...."

- ☐ "I get ticked off that no one ever told me this (better way to do things) when I first started teaching kids."

## And Now, These Messages....

Why do we want staff to hear us say the above statements? Because they send important messages to staff:

- ☐ we consider ourselves "works in progress"

- ☐ we are humble and honest

- ☐ we don't think that we know everything

- ☐ we don't think we are perfect

- ☐ even though we have lots of experience, that doesn't mean that we stop trying to get better

- ☐ we have learned and continue to learn a lot from watching and listening to other people

- ☐ some ways are better than others and it's important to evaluate and try different things to figure out what gets the best results

- ☐ we're persistent; we don't give up

- ☐ we have high standards and we hold ourselves to those standards

- ☐ we don't think that because we're the boss we don't have to keep learning and working hard

## Tactful Tactics

Suppose please that a supervisor said to a staff person, "The way you're getting these kids to line up for this game just doesn't work.

123

Here's how you do it...." We can see how some staff might think to themselves, "Oh, here comes Mr. or Ms. 'Expert' to enlighten me again...."

Now let's look at how a supervisor can use some facilitating phrases and some tact to approach the staff person in a way that is less likely to provoke defensiveness or insecurity. The supervisor might say, "You know, I've tried to get kids to line up for games like this, and some of the things I've tried have worked better than others. This can be a hard thing to get them to do. But I've watched how other leaders make it happen and I've changed how I do this. I think you'll like this much better—can I show you?" And then the supervisor can walk over to the campers with the staff person and add, "I get ticked off that nobody told me this when I first started, because this is so much easier to do than the way I used to do it..."

Please notice how the supervisor says that getting kids to line up is *hard*. That's a very smart thing to say out loud. It's not only true, but it takes some of the "sting" out of the fact that the staff person is having trouble doing it. Look also, please, at all the non-threatening messages that the supervisor sent: I don't think you're stupid; I used to have trouble with the same thing; I didn't figure this out by myself—I learned it by watching others; there's a way to do this that will make you happier....

When suggesting a new skill to a staff person, it's very effective when supervisors can identify the source of the "better way to do things" as someone other than themselves. When we mention how or where or from whom we learned how to do something, then it doesn't look like we're showing off how "brilliant" we are, because we're giving credit to others.

## Tact-ical Approaches

Here are some more facilitating phrases that help us make positive approaches to staff who are not doing things the way we want them done.

I like to say: "I have some ideas/thoughts about XYZ (the problem or situation), and I wanted to know, if I tell you about them, would you be willing to tell me what you think?"

Here, instead of just coming out and saying what I think, I'm asking the staff person to agree in advance to listen to what I say and communicate with me about it. Why do I ask staff to tell me what they think when I know that in most cases they will do it without my asking? Because I am letting them know right away that I am respectful—I don't expect to do all the talking. I'm saying that this will be a two-way process and that I want to hear what they feel about this situation.

This way, my views aren't shoved in their face. And because I'm asking them to contribute, they say "OK" in response to the question, or will nod or shrug, indicating that I can go ahead.

These are also effective ways to encourage communication in non-threatening ways:

- ☐ "I'd like to *learn* more about what you think about XYZ."
- ☐ "I would like your help in figuring out how we could best handle this..."

I used to ask staff, "In your opinion, what do you think about X?" Over the years I've experimented a bit and changed how I ask this, and I like this way better: "In your *experience*, what do you think about X?" Or, "In your *experience*, what do you think would happen if we tried it this way?" I learned to use the word "experience" when approaching older staff, or staff who were teachers or had otherwise worked with children for years. Anyone can have an "opinion," whether they know what they are talking about or not. The word "experience" shows that I acknowledge and respect their—well, experience.

## Anticipating Apprehensions

My major in college was speech communication. One of the many "use-it-every-day-of-your-life" things that I learned was the importance of stating anticipated objections out loud, right up front. This lets people know that we are aware of and sensitive to their feelings—that we are making sincere efforts to understand them and look at things not just from our perspective, but from their own.

So I've learned to say: "Carla, I'm concerned/worried/wondering that if I talk to you about XYZ (the problem or situation), that you'll think that I'm _____ ..." Into the blank goes what-

125

ever negative feelings I am guessing Carla might have. For example: "acting bossy," "acting like your mother," "putting my nose where it doesn't belong," "messing with something that you don't think is my business," or "talking about something that you already know."

Often, the staff person will shrug or shake their head to indicate that these thoughts never came to their mind. But people will often *say* that they weren't thinking something even when they were. In such cases, or even in instances where they really didn't have these thoughts, our efforts to show concern about their feelings will help to build trust and demonstrate respect.

That's the key word to remember: respect. Which is exactly what we want staff to remember when working with our children.

## Chapter Seventeen

# Help Campers Who Need Extra Support

We are well familiar with the camp rule, "Swim with a buddy." If we were serving as a lifeguard and we saw a child swimming alone in a lake, alarms would go off in our head and we would take immediate action to secure that child's safety.

*Our job as supervisors includes the responsibility to look for children who are "swimming alone" on dry land.* These are campers who have not made positive connections with others or who may not be enjoying camp as much as they could. Of course, staff will be bringing such campers to our attention. But on *Path 5 we make a proactive effort to look for unconnected or unhappy campers who may not have been noticed by other staff.*

All camp supervisors should be what I call "strifeguards." Strife usually applies to visibly violent struggles and other fights. But many children struggle with life "inside" themselves and have very real internal battles with loneliness, ostracism, exclusion, fears, and other difficult issues and feelings.

So when we walk Path 5, we look for children who are:

- □ having trouble making friends or haven't made any friends
- □ having difficulties interacting positively with others

- [ ] frequently excluded by other children
- [ ] almost never picked as partners or given other choice roles in a group
- [ ] often walking alone between activities
- [ ] often sitting alone or at some distance from everybody else
- [ ] not enjoying all or many parts of the camp experience
- [ ] having unusually difficult problems adjusting to being away from home
- [ ] showing an unusual amount of irritability
- [ ] often sitting out of activities

There are, of course, other possible signs of children who need some extra attention. We just need to be alert and vigilant, just as we would if we were guarding the water or a ropes course.

And please note—*we're not just looking for campers who are "drowning" in very serious problems*. We're also looking for campers who are not experiencing and enjoying the full range of benefits that camp has to offer. Which means, for example, that if a child is having a good time in all of the sports activities but will not participate in any crafts, singing, drama, and other non-athletic areas, we need to explore why that is and do whatever possible to broaden the camp experience for that young person.

## Collecting Information

The very first thing we do when we notice a camper who may need extra support is collect more information. We check in with that camper's counselor to get her or his perspective on how the child is doing. We should also visit specialist areas and speak with staff who are familiar with the camper.

We may also decide to check in with parents. They may have noticed something that will be helpful, or there may be things happening at home that could affect the child's camp experience.

Please learn from a serious mistake I made as a camp supervisor: never, ever assume that all parents will tell you things that you need to know to best support and serve their child. While most parents do provide full and helpful communication, there are some that do not.

I will never forget being an assistant day camp director and dealing with a boy who was behaving erratically for an entire morning. This was a young man who had pretty serious behavior problems on a "normal" day, but on this particular day he was truly uncontrollable. We called home at lunch and discovered that his father had passed away the prior evening; he had sat down in a recliner with a newspaper and collapsed. The stricken family had sent the boy to camp in some well-intentioned effort to preserve a little sanity in their just-collapsed world, but no one had called us so we could prepare for these exceptional circumstances.

This is, of course, an extreme example, but remembering it has always helped me keep in mind that children are products of their home environments, and when we see them at camp we are looking at only the tip of the proverbial iceberg. And "iceberg" is often the right metaphor, because there may be chilling things going on at home that parents may not tell us about because of embarrassment or because they feel that we do not need to know.

Remember that camper this morning that was making us understandably impatient? She might have been awakened last night by shouting and walked into a high-volume conversation between her parents that included the word "divorce."

At day camps, of course, events at home have a daily influence. At resident camps, the effect is different, but sometimes parents will communicate things in mail that may unintentionally upset their children.

I remember working for several days with a child who had become increasingly pensive and unmotivated. It was very helpful to speak with the parents and learn that a grandmother had just moved in with the family. The grandmother was unable to care for herself and the camper told me that he was afraid that his grandma would die, which was a fear he had not shared with his parents. With this information, camp and parents were able to work together to help the child understand that his feelings made perfect sense, and to provide him the extra love and support that he especially needed at that time.

## Don't Forget the Children as a Prime Source of Information

Interestingly, we sometimes forget to speak directly to the camper. I know this may seem strange, but there are many times when a group of adults try feverishly, with the best of intentions, to figure out a plan to help a child, without ever asking the child how she or he is feeling about the situation.

Children will often "open up" to supervisors. When supervisors regularly visit groups to have fun and establish themselves as warm, trustworthy people, campers will sometimes find it easier to speak to the supervisor than to their own counselor. Sometimes campers are embarrassed to have their counselor know about their feelings or may feel that they need someone else's help to make things right.

## Second Sight

Supervisors can and should act like a second pair of eyes and ears to interpret what is happening in a camper group. The supervisors' experience working with campers and their perspective from "outside" the group may help them notice important things.

Supervisors should note that sometimes counselors won't mention children who are not fitting in or who may not be having the best time. Why? In some cases, this can be because a counselor does not want that fact to be interpreted as a sign that the counselor is not being successful. Sadly, if the counselor doesn't speak up, such children then "fall through the cracks" and may not get the extra attention they need unless a vigilant, strife-guarding supervisor spots that child and dives in.

## Respecting the Counselor

It's important for us to respect a counselor's authority. Before intervening directly with the child, we should speak with the counselor and discuss the child's needs. Otherwise, the extra attention that we give to the child may be misinterpreted by a staff person as a statement that we do not think the staff person can handle this. The truth is that many children need additional support from more than one adult, and that's exactly how these situations should be approached when speaking with staff. Counselors will very much appreciate any assistance a supervisor can provide when it's presented as "support" and not as "taking over."

## But I'm Not a Shrink!

Few teachers have psychology degrees. Most parents don't. And I'm guessing that the majority of people in camping administration do not, although if degrees were given for experience, there would be a lot of camp directors with the option of charging by the hour.

We don't need to be psychologists to help children who are facing challenges and should not, if you will pardon the expression, shrink from our responsibilities to help.

Most of the children spotted by us on this Path can be helped enormously with just a little extra care and attention. Being sure to say hello to these children and engaging them in conversation can go a long way to helping them feel more secure.

Sometimes supervisors can devote time for some one-on-one listening or problem-solving that a counselor, who is responsible for the entire group, cannot.

There are many supervisors who have discovered that just going to drama with a "drama-reluctant" camper and enthusiastically participating with them can make all of the difference in motivating a child to try new things.

## But Don't Some of These Kids Have Problems That Are Beyond Our Abilities?

Yes. It is a fact that some of our campers could benefit from professional counseling. It's not our role to provide that. Our job is to do our best, within the limits of our experience and the resources of our camp, to provide children with the best possible support and guidance. If we feel that we are not making progress, or if we feel that a child's circumstances are making it difficult to serve other children, then we should speak to our camp director, ask for more ideas, and make a plan. Some camps retain social workers or psychologists or other consultants, just as schools do, who can provide additional advice and support in special cases.

However, having said all of this, it must still be acknowledged that camp is not for every child all of the time. This means that there are some children whose needs or circumstances at a particular time in a particular summer cannot be reasonably met by our camp. When these situations arise, the camp director sometimes has to make the painful decision that camp is not the best place for this child at this time. The reason we say "at this time" is because, with additional maturity, skills, care, or a different situation at home, a child may be able to fit in and enjoy camp at a later time.

Saying that camp can't meet every young person's needs at every time in her or his life shouldn't be understood as a rejection of a child, but instead as a practical assessment of a camp's resources. We wish we could help all children all of the time, but that's just not realistic.

## Ironing Out an Ironic Problem

So it's the first week in July and you've spotted a child who needs extra attention. You spend some very productive time speaking with this camper one-on-one over a period of several days. You are a world-class listener. You are fun to be with. Since this child, sadly, is not used to this kind of high-quality, uninterrupted attention, the child's energy and attitude revive immediately, much like a plant that receives its first delicious drenching after days of drought.

The ironic problem is that sometimes, after you work to help a child fit back into the group, the child weighs how much his or her needs are being met by you as opposed to the group and the group counselor, and you "win." When you establish a positive special relationship with campers, they will sometimes leave their group and run over to you when they see you coming.

Some of these campers will be satisfied with brief, happy inter-actions with you and then comfortably return to their group. But others will rather spend time with you. And where this really gets hairy is when some campers deliberately (or sometimes uncon-sciously) act badly or become sullen just so that they can be "sent" to you, where they get another powerful dose of reinforcing attention.

## The Solution to Sticky Campers

So what's the solution to this? Obviously, you need to be brutally cold in your one-on-one interactions with such children, demolish their self-esteem, tell them that you find young people highly annoying and are only doing this camp thing to rake in the big bucks for early retirement, and send them back to their group.

Sorry. It's late at night, I'm getting a little punchy, and I couldn't resist that. Let me try this again....

So what's the solution to this? It's a tricky problem, but it's best solved by being aware that it can arise and by taking these steps:

First, we need to let campers we work with *know* that we want them to be a part of their group—that it would please us, as their friend, to see them having a great time.

Second, we need to be both gentle and firm about the time we spend one-on-one with campers and speak to them about this out loud. This is no different than the balancing act done by all good parents who want to shower highly beneficial attention on their children but also want to teach them to be independent. We can say something like, "You don't want to go now because you like talking and spending time with me. That's good! That means we're friends and we know we can trust each other, which is a great thing.

"But because we're friends, that means you have to help me just like I help you. I have to go do some other things and work with some other people right now because that's my job at camp. I'd like to spend more time talking with you now but that's not an option. I can check with you later, but I need you to help me now by going back to your group and doing your best, and then I promise that I'll check on you later and I hope you'll be able to tell me that things are better...."

We should be specific with campers about what "doing your best" means. We should figure out a plan with the camper that includes specific steps that the camper can take to *make* things better. The counselor should be included in these discussions.

*Finally, it's important to repeatedly refer back to the group counselor in your discussions with the camper.* Please remember that our goal is to help the camper build a successful relationship with the group counselor. We can say, "When things like XYZ happen or when you're feeling like ABC, I want you to tell your counselor, and I'll talk with your counselor so that she/he knows that you and I have talked about this...."

## Don't Forget Everyone Else

It's easy for a supervisor to get caught up in additional efforts to help unconnected children and forget some of the joys of just interacting generally with all of the campers. I've heard many supervisors complain about how exhausting it can be working from hour to hour with campers that are hard for others to handle. So please be sure to balance how you spend your time so that you are enjoying and participating with all types of children. Plus, remember that when working with the most challenging campers, we don't need to do this alone. Which brings us to....

## The Pathways Meeting

You might want to review Chapter Eleven, where we spoke about helping staff be positive and patient when working with children who pose challenges. Just as we want staff to know how much we appreciate their extra efforts for challenging kids, we should communicate the same messages to ourselves. And we should use the Pathways meetings to get support and new ideas so that our work with unconnected children is a team effort.

## The Power

I'll let you in on a personal secret about why I use the "strife-guard" term. The water imagery helps remind me of children who are parched—thirsty for attention and love. But mostly, it makes me think of children in the water. Children like Danny. Please join me in the next chapter and you'll see why this image is so powerful for me.

## Chapter Eighteen

# Danny:
# The Power of Path 5

Danny was one of many campers that I kept an extra eye on as a camp administrator. He was tall for his nine years, had dark hair, and deep eyes. He sometimes had problems "fitting in" with others and his greatest demon was the swimming pool. He refused to enter it.

I tried making connections with Danny. I learned his name right away and made sure when saying hello to his group that I gave a little extra smile and eye contact to him. When campers in his group spoke to me about their interests or accomplishments, I would sometimes put my arm on Danny's shoulder, ask Danny if he'd heard about this (he'd shyly look down and shake his head "no") and ask the camper to tell *us* so that I could encourage some communication between others and Danny. Danny's counselor was great. As I had asked him, he made a particular point of coming up to me at times with Danny in tow, to report an accomplishment of Danny in order to boost his confidence and make sure he knew that he was noticed and appreciated. Of course, we did this with other campers, too, but we made a special point of being sure that Danny felt secure.

I sat with Danny a few times and asked him about swimming. At first he didn't want to talk about it. *But I learned the key skill of not asking him about swimming while we were at swimming.* When he was seated at the side of the pool with his clothes on, he was tense and felt worried that somebody would make him go in the water. So I looked for other opportunities during the day, when he was feeling stronger, to bring it up gently and see if I could find out more.

After about a week, I had begun to earn his trust, and Danny started to talk a little bit about swimming. He admitted that it scared him. I immediately told him, "Well then this makes perfect sense. You're so smart. I wouldn't want to go someplace that scared me." I still remember today how those deep, dark eyes of his showed surprise when I said that.

I'm sure he was expecting me to respond with, "Oh, is that all? Don't be silly, there's nothing for a big strong boy like you to be afraid of!" But that would have denied his feelings and made him feel stupid and embarrassed. Instead, I wanted Danny to know that I was very glad that he could talk to me about his fears, and that it was brave and smart for him to do so.

Danny and I had lunch together one day and I spoke with him about my own troubles with swimming when I was a camper. I explained to him how my counselors made me take my glasses off for swimming. I told him how hard it was for me to watch the instructors when I couldn't see them and how I was too shy to tell them this. I stood and squinted my eyes, my arms stretched out in front of me as though I were trying to find the pool. Danny grinned, ever so slightly.

When we work with children who are sad or lonely or scared, getting that one-second grin is like hitting a clean double with the bases loaded. We want to jump up and pump the air with our fist and yell "Yessss!" But, of course, instead we just smile back, while inside our head we jump up, pump the air, and yell "Yessss!"

Danny and I made a plan about swimming. In fact, we even wrote it down on an official-looking piece of blue camp stationery. It was a "deal" between Uncle Mike and Danny in which he promised to bring his suit the next day and I promised to do the same. He promised to go in the water the next day, and I promised that I would hold him and go in with him. If he was too uncomfortable, then we'd go back out together. Under no circumstances would I let go of him. We'd walk in a little and keep our heads completely out of the water. No swimming. We walk in. We walk out. Just checking out the pool.

Danny asked a lot of questions and we spelled everything out in our contract. I remember imagining a successful future for him as a mergers and acquisitions attorney.

The next day, we suited up for battle against demons. Danny clutched the blue paper on which we had recorded our agreement. I sat down with him in the pool changing area. That's what I was silently hoping—that it would really be a "changing" area. I asked Danny to tell me how he was feeling, and he did. I tried to let him know that he had just accomplished a great deal by putting on the bathing suit and that he must be feeling proud about that. I told him that I was proud of him, too. It's easy to be friends with people who can do easy things, I said, but the best friends to have are people who can try hard things. That, I explained, was why I respected him so much.

And then we stepped into the shallowest part of the pool. He stood facing me. I picked him up and he wrapped his arms around my neck. I specifically remember how tightly he was holding on to me—it didn't seem possible that such strength could come from just a young boy. We walked very slowly. I also remember how quiet people became around us. They, too, knew that this was a big moment. I kept whispering in Danny's ear to remind him that there was no way I was letting go, no matter what. We walk in. We walk out. Just checking out the pool.

We stopped when the water wrapped over my shoulders. Danny had been straining and stretching his neck to get his head above even my own. We stood there, quietly, neither of us speaking. And then, after we'd been standing together for a moment, I felt the ever-so-slight loosening of his grip and the relaxing of his neck. I saw the pride on his face. I felt moisture on my face. Not from the pool, but from my eyes. At that moment, there was no place on earth I would have rather been.

In the days that followed, Danny started to work—cautiously, but with a new attitude—with the swim counselors in the shallow end of the pool.

And then a few weeks later it was Water Fun Day, a pool-based special event. All the kids and staff were seated around the pool, ready for some creative relays. Uncle Ken, my boss, stood on one diving board and I stood on a parallel one. We were both wearing enormous, outrageously gaudy bathing shorts and were about to have a comic "race" around the pool. As we had rehearsed, Ken began to brag loudly about being the best swimmer at the camp, and I gently reminded him that it was not polite to be boastful; he could be proud of his swimming without saying he was better than other people.

"Besides," I added, "here at our camp, Uncle Ken, we have lots of terrific swimmers!" I hadn't planned on this, but as I looked over the water at those hundreds of faces, I suddenly picked one out. It was Danny. Wearing a swimming suit. Sitting with all the other campers. No longer alone.

And so I said, "For example, there's Danny B. over there. He's one of our hardest working swimmers!" His counselor clapped him on the back. Danny looked both surprised and proud.

I suppose if I had thought about doing this in advance, I would have analyzed it to death, worried about him being embarrassed, and not mentioned him at all.

Fast forward please, many, many years. I was doing a workshop for a very large group of camp counselors. We took a break. I was answering a young lady's question, she said thanks, and walked away. At that instant I felt a tap on my shoulder and turned around. I was looking at a man's collar bone. I had to turn my neck up to look at his face. He had been sitting in the very first row all morning, nodding, smiling, taking notes. I looked at the name tag on his shirt. Danny B.

My mouth began to widen in disbelief. He was saying, "I don't know if you'll remember me...." I was really quite stunned, and I blurted out: "I still have it!"

Now it was his turn to be stunned. I could tell immediately that he knew what I was talking about. "No way!" he said.

"I do, I swear it!" I replied. "I have it in a file at home. Blue paper. Camp stationery. Our swimming contract."

"You *saved* it?" he asked.

"Yes," I said.

He shook his head like he couldn't believe this. He said, "Well,

I just wanted you to know that I still remember the day you were on that diving board and you mentioned my name as one of the swimmers. I couldn't believe that out of all the kids at camp, my name was the one that you mentioned. I can't tell you what that did for me—how that made me feel—but I wanted to thank you."

He went on for a moment to explain that he had felt a little lost back then, and how he had faced some significant challenges for some years afterwards as a young adult. He said that even now that he was older, he still thought back many times to that day on which he had been acknowledged at the pool.

It was hard for me to know what to say. I had not known, of course, that this spontaneous comment had had such an impact on him. We spoke for a few more moments.

Then I said, "So, Danny, what are you doing here?"

And I want you to hear what he said. He said, "I'm a counselor here. I'm you now."


So my message to you is this: please never forget that as a camp supervisor, even in a few seconds, you can make a difference in a child's life so significant that it may be remembered and appreciated by that child long enough to be repeated by them to their grandchildren.

Know that you have this power. And rejoice that we are in a position to use it to make lasting positive differences in the lives of children.

## Chapter Nineteen

# Keep Camp Safe

All supervisors know, even if we haven't been told directly, that one of our most important jobs is to "patrol" the camp and look out for things that are dangerous or otherwise unsafe.

With our SuperVision approach we can do even more. We're not only going to look for things that are currently unsafe, but we're going to do more proactive risk assessment and figure out what areas have a potential for being unsafe. And we'll do this every day as a regular part of our daily work on Path 6, not just when we happen to see something that makes us think about safety.

## The 360 Technique

Let's begin with an example of how we typically supervise for safety. We're walking past the barn building where we have drama activities and rainy day programming. As we approach the doorway, we see a nail end that has popped through the doorframe. It's not sticking out far, but it certainly could hurt someone if he or she fell against it. So we make a note to get someone with a hammer to pull the nail and replace it. This is good, standard supervision.

In our SuperVision system, we can expand our skills and do even more. We use a technique on Path 6 that I call the "360."

Here's how we do it. At least three times a day, whenever we'd like, we pick a place at camp and just stand still in it for about two minutes, slowly turning in a complete circle (*360* degrees). As we turn, we keep our eyes and ears alert, and instead of asking the usual supervision question—"Is there anything unsafe here?"— we ask the 360 question: "When something goes wrong here, *what will it be?*"

This question pushes us to be creative and think harder. It recognizes that every area of camp has a certain potential for risk.

## Barn to Be Wild

Now let's suppose that we're back at the barn. We haven't seen any evil nail. We just picked this area to do our 360 this morning.

We slowly turn while asking the question, "When something goes wrong here, what will it be?" And we just stand there for a moment, brainstorming.

The first thing we see as we turn are the railings that run alongside the ramp that leads up at an incline to the entrance to the barn. If someone were to get hurt on these railings, we ask, how would they do it, and what could we do to reduce the risk of injury? These are some things that we come up with:

☐   Kids might jump off the railings. We notice that on the ground below there are some pebbles and some larger, sharp-edged rocks. These could be moved. We could remind staff to be sure that campers know not to jump off the railings. We could speak with the drama specialist and ask if she or he has seen any such jumping, and ask the specialist to keep an eye out for it. We could also ask the specialist to make a colorful sign that reminds campers to please not jump or climb on the railings.

☐   Every supervisor knows that young people believe it is their daily duty to pull on, climb over, and swing under railings. They do this to test the crash worthiness of railings, and they must do this every day, just in case there were major structural changes to the railings during the prior night. As we look closely, we notice that some of the railings are not sanded smoothly on their underside; it will take only a few minutes with some sandpaper to quickly remove potential sliver-makers from both railings.

☐   As we continue to make our circle, we are now facing the barn doors themselves. Again we ask, when something goes wrong, what will it be? We know that kids like to swing on big doors, and push them open and closed, often while others are standing in the doorway. This can cause caught fingers, bumped heads, and so on. So this gives us the quick idea of securing the doors when they are open. A simple eye-hook or other fastener at adult height or higher would keep the open doors in place, eliminating any potential risk if a camper decided to take a ride on a door and sweep others out of the way while doing so.

So in just a few minutes of thinking, we've come up with some great additional ways to make camp safer. It's true that no camper has been hurt yet by any of the things that we observed. But by taking these easy-to-implement preventive steps, we greatly reduce the risk that they will be hurt. And that's the kind of proactive use of our daily time that walking Path 6 is all about.

## Field of Screams

Here's another example of a 360: On a camp consulting visit this past summer, I was watching several groups play different field games in a very large, open, grassy area. I asked myself the 360 question: When something goes wrong here, what will it be? I noticed something that I had not seen on a prior visit to this area. There was a pebble-covered, dusty road that ran alongside part of an area near where one of the groups was playing. Their game was an active one where players run quickly, often backwards, from a ball that has been thrown straight up in the air. I imagined that the thing that would go wrong here was that someone would trip and stumble on the hard rocks instead of the soft grass. We've all seen those shallow but nasty abrasion cuts that kids can get when they fall or slide on rocks or gravel. No one got hurt in this way while I was watching, but the 360 pushes us to think about problems before they happen.

So I joined the game for a few minutes, had fun, and then just mentioned to the group leader that we might move the whole game over about 50 yards to be farther from the road, just in case any of these super-fast runners in her group got a little too far away. The supervisor that I was walking around with made a note to keep an eye on this corner of the field and try to remind staff to move closer to the center to avoid any problems.

## Hazard Hikes

You don't have to do the 360 alone. Take another supervisor with you. It only takes a moment. Walk out to a spot and start looking around. I sometimes call these "Hazard Hikes." Brainstorming with someone else is more interesting and it often yields better results. Two doom predictors are better than one.

## Safety Inside and Out

I like to think of safety at camp in two ways: outside safety and inside safety.

Outside safety means "physical" safety—keeping people from getting bumped, cut, bruised, or otherwise bodily injured. Given the large number of children at our camps who are engaged in active play every season, I think our overall safety record in camping is something to be truly proud of. And by walking this Path and using our 360 rule, we can do even better.

Inside safety deserves our equal attention. Inside safety means "psychological" or "emotional" safety. It means protecting our children from damage to their feelings that is inflicted intentionally or even unknowingly by others.

We're not talking about making camp a "utopia" where no one's feelings get hurt. First, that's not possible, and second, that's not our goal. When campers lose a game or don't get picked to do something that they want, they need to learn how to handle these feelings, and camp is a terrific, supportive environment to do so.

When I speak about inside safety, I'm talking about creating a camp atmosphere where everyone works on eliminating put-downs, cruel teasing, taunting, ridicule, and other demeaning and degrading behavior. In workshops, I ask attendees to raise their hands if they knew someone in school who was a regular "target" of such negative behavior. Nearly everyone raises their hand. I'm betting that you knew of such people, too. I then ask, "How many of you believe that some of the people in this room are raising their hand because they themselves were such targets?" All the hands go up.

Next question: "Please picture that person or persons right now. How many of you believe that as a result of being such a target, the lives of these people were damaged or limited in ways that might still affect them even today?" All of the hands go up again to acknowledge this truth.

Finally, I ask them, and I now ask you: "Suppose we could go back in time. Suppose one of us could find these "target people" and support them and teach them how to cope, and work with the people doing the damage to let them know that they were hurting others, that this was not acceptable, and teach them how to relate to people in less hurtful ways. If we did that, how many of you believe that the lives of those target people would be fundamentally changed in positive ways forever?" When the hands go up, I like to look into people's eyes. I see them recognizing the power they have right now to help make camp a culture in which demeaning and degrading behavior is firmly kept out.

To achieve this goal, we will train our staff to notice put-downs or "dissing" (short for disrespect). "You're a loser." We will teach them not to ignore such statements and to understand that they are serious and do not belong at camp. "Stupid." Even if people say that they are "kidding" we tell them that this kind of teasing is just not the way we treat each other and that it isn't allowed.

Put-downs flourish in places where people ignore them or just treat them as the supposedly "normal" way kids talk to each other. What most often happens is that the minor teasing expands into constant hammering at certain kids. We've all read in newspapers and seen on television what can happen when one young person or a group of young people are increasingly isolated in this way. Often, their frustration can turn to violent behavior, against others as well as themselves.

## The 360 Plus

We can help keep the camp environment safe "inside" by using a simple technique that I call the 360 Plus. It's "Plus" because we now expand our vision to look for emotional hazards.

Just as we stood in one place and applied our experience and imagination to find out what we could do to make an area safer physically, we can do the same thing for "inside" safety. When we walk around camp, we look for places in which put-down behavior is more likely to take place. I call these "petri places"— named after those circular glass petri dishes we had in science class in which bacteria and other gross-looking stuff would grow in a culture that supported them.

Here's a hint about where to find petri places. I've found that the places where negative and abusive talk grow fastest at camp are in the informal locations where groups of campers gather. In these places, campers may not be as closely supervised because staff often use these opportunities to talk with each other and may pay less attention to what is going on with the children. Examples of these places include changing rooms for swimming, gathering places where campers and staff wait for things to get started, and areas outside a dining hall where they wait to go in for a meal.

As supervisors, it's our job to keep our vigilance up where staff vigilance may be down. We must keep alert for negative and abusive talk and look for people who may be "targets." We represent the camp and the director and have even greater power than staff to set the right expectations for inside safety. It's a strong thing when we take a stand and say to campers, kindly but firmly, "We don't go there" or "We don't like that kind of stuff here at camp. Everybody's safe."

## How Do We Make Sure That We Are Doing a Good Job on This Path?

We'll talk about what we've seen and done on Path 6 at our regular Pathways meetings with our director. We'll explain that we've spoken to someone about securing the barn doors, moving some rocks, and doing some quick sanding. (We did this right away, of course; we didn't wait for our Pathways meeting to initiate safety actions.) We can discuss ideas or concerns that we have about outside and inside safety. For example, if we've noticed that there is a lack of supervision while campers gather in the morning, we can talk about how to speak with staff about improving this, and make some plans with other supervisors to do some teaching by example as we show staff the importance of sitting with their campers and keeping them occupied with conversation or games.

## Summary

When we are walking on Path 6, we're proactively analyzing risks and focusing on prevention. And we're thinking not just about physical safety, but how people are feeling inside. Let's always remember: when someone falls down on a rocky path, their abrasions will probably heal quickly. But the bruising campers may get on the inside from the cruel or negative talk of others may take much longer to heal. And as many of us know, sometimes it never heals at all. This can motivate us to keep our level of vigilance high and work hard to make a strong and long-lasting difference in the lives of our children.

## Chapter Twenty

# Pathways Meetings: 10 Tips

We first described the Pathways meetings in Chapter Four. These are regular weekly meetings we have with our director (or someone else who is *our* supervisor) to talk about our work on the six Paths. Here are ten things that we can do to help make these meetings a success:

1.  **Set the meeting for the same time each week.** Even if the meeting needs to be rescheduled sometimes due to other important matters, having this regularly scheduled time blocked out in advance is much more efficient than trying to schedule a different time every week and it makes it much more likely that the meeting will occur. Scheduling and having a Pathways meeting at least once a week ensures that there is regular communication about achieving important camp goals.

2.  **Prepare in advance what we are going to talk about at the meeting.** These meetings are informal and shouldn't be treated as formal "reports." But to make the best use of everyone's time, we shouldn't just walk in and try to figure out what we're going to say. If we do,

directors will be justified in asking us to come back later after we've thought things through. Directors should and will evaluate how well we are doing our job in large part based on how well prepared we are for these meetings.

3. **Bring some notes that summarize what we've done for each Path.** We can use these notes as "talking points" for the meeting. For Path 1, for example, which deals with creative programming, we would jot down variations or new ideas we've introduced and tried with groups. When do we do this jotting? Please see the next point....

4. **Make brief notes every day about what we've done on the Paths.** If we sit at a picnic table a half hour before the meeting and try to think up a bunch of stuff to say, this will make us miserable and feel like busywork. To make the SuperVision system work, we have to be thinking about the Paths every day. With just a little practice and discipline, we'll be jotting notes to ourselves every day to keep track of what we're doing in each of the six areas.

   You might find it helpful to create a note-taking sheet that lists the six Paths and has space for you to write some comments each day as you prepare for the Pathways meeting. This becomes a great tool to use during the meeting itself.

5. **We should not get hung up on whether something fits more properly in one Path as opposed to another.** It doesn't really matter; in fact, some actions that we take may fit in more than one Path. The Paths are set up as general guidelines to help us focus our efforts on what's most important.

6. **If we don't have something to say about every Path every week, it's OK.** If this happens, our director will just ask us to be guided by this fact as we work to increase our activities on every Path in the days that follow. The SuperVision system is designed to help us evaluate how we are spending our time and assist us in making sure that

we are using our talents in all of the important areas, not just a few.

7.  **Always try to talk about the Paths first before discussing other matters.** We may have other issues to discuss or questions to ask during the time we've scheduled for the Pathways meeting. It's OK, of course, to speak about these other things, but if we don't begin with the Paths, there's a good chance that we won't have enough time to finish our Paths conversation, or our meeting may get interrupted before we get to the Paths.

8.  **Build an underground cavern and hold Pathways meetings deep within it.** If a cavern isn't available, we should at least try to have the meeting someplace other than the camp office. We want to be away from phones and out of a heavy traffic pattern to maximize the chance that we will be able to say three sentences in a row before a counselor comes up and asks if it would be OK if the campers ride the horses without helmets today because it's just so darned hot....

9.  **Ask questions.** I feel sad that the extensive experience of so many highly-skilled camp directors and senior administrators gets shared with supervisors so infrequently. Often, this sharing happens only when there is some big problem, or when a supervisor doesn't handle something in the best possible way. *Then* the supervisor gets the benefit of some coaching and expert advice. It shouldn't be that way. Indeed, one of the main reasons I came up with the Pathways meeting is to give directors an opportunity to share their expertise on a regular, positive basis. These meetings are terrific opportunities to do this. Nothing teaches us faster or better than having a mentor. Asking questions about how to handle situations lets us learn a lot from those who have so much experience to share.

10. **There's no special reason that these meetings should be only once a week.** I certainly wouldn't have them less frequently, but at some camps you may find that meeting more often is very helpful. If you're at a not-for-profit

camp that runs for only one short session, you'll have to work on scheduling a few brief meetings to get as much communication going as you can.

## An Example: Kayla's Pathways Meeting

After a moment of small talk, camp supervisor Kayla takes out this week's six Paths note sheet and begins talking to her director about Path 1. She describes the work that she's done with some fourth and fifth grade girls groups to liven up things at field sports. She gives some brief examples and explains that her favorite was at soccer, when she had the girls link arms in groups of four or five. The girls had to move the ball around without letting go of each other. Kayla explains how this forced the girls to work on teamwork, especially on talking with each other to coordinate efforts. So often in team sports, Kayla says, many kids don't talk to each other enough, or at all, about how they can work together. So Kayla had the girls try this linked arm activity without allowing them to speak at all. The girls quickly discovered that it was much harder without fully communicating. Kayla spoke with the group counselors about why she insisted on trying this in silence first so that the girls would more greatly value talking to each other when it was allowed.

The depth of Kayla's thinking really impresses the director, and the director says so. This wasn't just a creative change to make the activity more interesting; it also served as a terrific teaching tool.

As Kayla looks down at her notes for a few seconds to decide what to say next, the director silently realizes that without the structure of a regular Pathways meeting, it might have been awkward for Kayla to talk about her success. What excuse could she have used to bring it to the director's attention? Would Kayla have been concerned that she would have appeared to be "tooting her own horn" if she brought it up in the course of some other conversation? In the Pathways meetings, we're *supposed* to talk about successes and challenges and no "excuse" is necessary. Plus, the director concludes, the meeting provides a perfect chance to give Kayla some well-deserved recognition.

Kayla continues to discuss what she has done on the remaining

Paths. She confesses that she hasn't done as much as she would like on Path 5, but she says that she's going to concentrate on some "strifeguarding" in the next day or so.

When she gets to Path 3, Kayla brings the director up to date on her work with a group counselor that has been having trouble motivating her older girls group. Kayla had tried something that the director suggested last week and she asks for some additional ideas, which the director provides.

Kayla also mentions that she walked by swimming several times in the last few days and has some concerns. Some of the instructors are working with only one child at a time without doing anything to keep the other children involved while they are waiting for their turn. The director thanks her for mentioning it and will make a point of visiting swimming and speaking with the aquatics supervisor to look into this further.

Once the Paths discussion is complete, there is some additional conversation about preparations for the upcoming special event. The director then ends the meeting in a positive way by pointing out that Kayla had specific examples of things that she did on five of the six Paths, which really shows she is working hard on important things in a variety of areas. The director also notes that Kayla keeps following up on matters that they had discussed in earlier meetings.

## Teaming with Success

Regular Pathways meetings help directors and supervisors work effectively as a team to support staff in doing their best possible work to serve our children.

## Chapter Twenty-One

# Leading Effective Staff Meetings

Staff meetings are often treated basically as convenient opportunities to communicate information to all staff at the same time. But they can be so much more.

Short, well-prepared, skillfully led meetings can motivate, provide additional training, boost team spirit, and set a positive, energetic tone for staff as they return to their campers.

## Have Regular Short Meetings

Meeting with staff on a regular basis is *very* important. Depending on the size of your staff and your goals for the meetings, you may have all-staff meetings or meet in units or other sub-groups. There are, of course, no rules as to how often such meetings should be held, but I would suggest holding brief meetings at least once or twice a week at five-day-a-week camps and at least three times per week at seven-day-a-week camps.

At the end of this chapter, I've included some fun ideas for keeping the campers occupied while you meet with staff.

How long should such meetings be? Meetings called for special purposes might take longer, but quick five to ten minute meetings can produce lots of benefits. Even getting a unit of counselors or specialists together in a quick group huddle for two fast points of communication and a "hands-in-the-middle" cheer, like a football team about to run a play, can do a lot to begin a day with more direction, spirit, and energy.

I should quickly interrupt to note here that I worked years ago at a camp where, sadly, the directors didn't want to have staff meetings because they were concerned they would turn into "gripe sessions." This was most unfortunate. Properly led meetings would not have invited such problems and would have provided great positive opportunities to build a stronger staff team.

## Making Meetings Positive

Too often, some staff meetings feature an administrator reading from a clipboard a list of problems that have arisen since the last meeting.

- ☐ "Stay on the schedule...."

- ☐ "Don't let your campers wander from the group...."

- ☐ "Please, staff, do be aware of strangers on the grounds. But when you see an unfamiliar adult coming up the path, do not wrestle them to the ground and ask if you can help them—first ask if you can help them, and *then* wrestle them to the ground...."

Instead of listing problems or mistakes that need to be corrected, we should try whenever possible to handle them positively by identifying things that we *value*. Instead of saying "There are a lot of campers that are wandering from their groups...." we can say "We really want you to know how much we appreciate it when you keep everyone in your group together." In place of "You must stay on the schedule...." we can say instead, "We needed to find a camper yesterday right away, in response to a parent phone call, and we were able to do this in less than two minutes for only one reason—because that camper's group was exactly where it was supposed to be, right on schedule."

There are some times, of course, when we need to directly address certain problems. The point is that we should also be using these meetings as opportunities to praise and celebrate positive staff choices that are contributing to success.

## More Tips for Making the Most Out of Meetings

☐ **Start with something strongly positive;** don't just read items from a list in whatever order they've been noted. For example, tell about a terrific sign of super staff that you've observed (please refer to Chapter Seven and "SOSS: Xcellent Xamples" in the Liver for help with this). Motivate staff by sharing with them a brief portion of a thank you letter or summaries of phone calls received from grateful parents. Announce an achievement by a camper (first time in the water after some earlier reluctance, or successful climbing of the big wall, and so on). Use these to emphasize the positive differences staff make in the lives of children every day.

☐ **Present a "Skill of the Day,"** as explained in Chapter Eight.

☐ **Have two-minute "skill shares."** If someone has come up with a great game for groups to play during transition periods, have this staff person summarize or show it. If a specialist has found it really effective to involve kids in the demonstration of a technique, have the specialist show how this is done. The "skill shares" are, of course, a terrific way to give recognition to the staff members who present them.

☐ **Present a "challenge of the day"**—a common problem with some suggested solutions.

☐ **Present information in a prepared, organized manner.** We want to avoid this: "Jan is going to tell us about—Jan, are you here?—OK, Jan is going to tell us about Water Fun Day on Friday.... What? Oh. OK, well before Jan—huh? OK, well why don't we just have Bo talk about it and then—what? OK, well Star says we're not calling it Water Fun Day, but here's Bo to tell you about it. Where is Bo?...."

☐ **Prepare your conclusion in advance**, just as you prepared a good opening. It may be only one or two sentences, but we don't want to end these meetings with a hastily remembered announcement about wet towels left on the floor of changing areas or people putting spoons in the sudsy bin for forks. We want to be sure that everyone leaves on an upbeat, positive note. For a more effective conclusion, try these examples:

- End with a positive quote about leadership or other subjects related to camp.

- Start a tradition of asking one staff person to present their hope or goal for the day (these should not be jokes and should be prepared in advance), such as "My hope is that every camper connects in some way with someone new today, either as a partner, or just by having a conversation, or by sitting next to somebody different at lunch."

- Consider concluding with a staff cheer, as a sports team might.

- Again, you can use a comment from a parent or camper that reminds everyone of the importance of their work.

## Making Time for Meetings

There is always time for brief, effective meetings at every camp. Finding this time, especially in a day camp setting where opportunities may seem more limited, can be challenging at first. We just have to be a little creative sometimes. Let me please show you one fast and easy way to get this done.

Almost all camps already have some large group assemblies or other all-camp gatherings. It might be first thing in the morning when flags are raised, announcements are made, and songs are sung. There may be similar events at the end or at other times of the day, including meals.

Quick meetings can be held during these times when staff are already together. One or two administrators, specialists, or other staff with strong large group leadership skills can hold the attention of big groups of campers while the rest of staff hustle someplace very close by for a quick huddle.

But here's the simple but important trick to making this work. Begin the gathering with campers and staff together. Do whatever you would normally do at the gathering. This allows the usual momentum to be built and gives staff the opportunity to be sitting with the campers, modeling appropriate behavior and participation. Then, when things are going smoothly, we can pull staff out for a quick meeting while the campers continue the program with one or two leaders.

## Fun Things for Campers to Do While Staff Are Away for a Few Moments

We can of course use special songs, games, stunts, stories, and so on to keep campers involved and entertained. But from time to time we can also use the very fact that staff are away as a special program element that will keep the children motivated even though their counselors are not there. Here are some examples of what the one or two remaining leaders can do:

□ The campers can plan and practice something as a secret to be presented when the staff return. This can be a new song that the staff will be "stunned" that the campers have learned. (We explain the "act stunned" part to staff at our meeting.) In fact, when everyone is back together again, the director or someone else can begin teaching the song to the campers, "believing" that the campers do not already know it. Nothing—and I mean *nothing*—motivates campers more than when they are able to be smarter than the adults.

□ As a "joke" on the director, campers can be taught the answers to challenging questions that the director will be asking when returning with the other staff from the meeting. The director, of course, is "amazed" at their ability to answer.

□ The campers learn to respond in a funny way to a secret word. For example, the kids are told that assistant director Ski will return from the quick meeting and talk about the upcoming special event. Whenever Ski says the word "water," every camper will jump up and sing the first two lines of "My Bonnie Lies Over the Ocean" while pretending to swim. Ski acts mystified as to why this is happening, and once again the campers have a riot because they know something that a grown up doesn't.

The trick to making this really fun, by the way, is for Ski to "almost" say the word several times before actually saying it. In other words, Ski says, "Wow, my throat is so dry, I really need a glass of—(Ski pauses, as if trying to think of a word)." The kids, expecting the imminent use of the word "water," are ready to jump out of their skin, but Ski says "juice." Then a few moments later, Ski refers to swimming and the pleasure on a hot day of "jumping into the cool, clear, refreshing—(pause) liquid stuff."

In the above example, Ski was secretly aware of what was going on, but it's also fun to do this secret word thing when the person up front is not in on the joke.

☐ The secret word can be a gesture instead. Every time Ski puts a hand on a hip, for example, campers can erupt in a planned response.

☐ You can also do this as a game, where the campers know the secret word, Ski doesn't, and Ski tries to guess it. You can give Ski a subject matter as a clue and Ski can ask 20 questions or just talk a lot about that subject, hoping to say it.

☐ Campers can practice super-loud singing that will, when presented to staff, "cause" them (they've been secretly cued for this in advance) to go into fetal positions with ears covered.

It's smart for the leader to establish hand signals in advance that will cue the campers to stop singing or return to a lower volume.

They can also practice singing a song so softly that returning staff (again, secretly prepared) have to keep shouting "What?!" to hear what's being sung. Super slow or super fast singing is fun for them to practice, too, as a surprise for staff and the person who returns from the meeting to lead the song.

☐   Campers pair up, look at each other for a minute, and then stand with their backs facing their partners. Everyone changes three things about their appearance. They put a watch on an opposite wrist, hide their socks in their pockets, and so on. Then they face their partner and try to identify the three changes that their partner made. Just before staff return from their meeting, the campers can change things about their appearance one more time, and staff can try to guess what changes the campers made.

☐   Staff who have been meeting can plan a surprise of their own for campers upon their return. They can change their appearance, plan a response to a secret word or gesture, and so on.

## Chapter Twenty-Two

# Modeling & The Pass Down Principle

I discussed what I call the "PDP"—the pass-down principle—in Chapter Fourteen of *Training Terrific Staff,* and it is very relevant to our daily conduct as supervisors. Basically, the pass-down principle says that *the way administrators work with staff and campers becomes a model for how staff will work with the children.*

## Tone Check

The way we speak to everyone at camp becomes a model of how staff should speak to their campers and to each other. If we're sarcastic, for example, or abrupt, or put others down, then the message gets sent that these are OK ways to speak. An administrator who never—or only intermittently—says "please" will have greater difficulties getting staff to be respectful to campers. Supervisors who are often brusque when giving directions to campers ("I said line up, let's go!" and "You call this a straight line?!") should not be surprised if some staff adopt this tone, too.

I was folding up my flip chart after an orientation workshop at an agency resident camp this past summer and overheard one of the division heads who was addressing a small group of staff.

When I had met her earlier in the day, I saw that she was a friendly, warm person. But as she was assigning cabins and clean-up duties to staff, I found it very interesting that her tone sounded pretty cold and "military." She said things like, "You *cannot* leave camp until you check out with me." Her very pleasant smile had disappeared. I wondered if she was adopting this stern tone because she was a young supervisor and *because* she was such a nice and likeable person. Was she concerned that staff might not respect her or take her seriously unless she sounded more "serious" or more like a "boss?"

## Second Example, Happy Ending

Ironically, the next morning I saw the same thing at a different location, but it was followed by a terrific example of getting the tone just right. This was a not-for-profit group of day camps from several different sites, and staff were to sign in as they arrived. Not all of them were doing this, so one of the supervisors started shouting across the room in a cold, somewhat harsh voice: "Listen up! Everybody *must* be signed in—if you have not done so, go back out into the hallway and do it right away so we can get started!" Well, OK, this wasn't horrible, but it certainly wasn't an example of the kind of warmth that we ask our staff to project when the children arrive. I also noticed that nobody seemed to be rushing to sign up.

A few minutes later, a different supervisor from one of the other sites jumped onto the stage and made the same announcement with quite a contrasting style. "Good morning, everybody!" he loudly sang out to the sleepy staff. When I say, "sang," I mean he actually sang. He was smiling and had his arms spread out as if he were trying to hug everybody in the room. The sleepy faces looked up. Then he said—and I immediately wrote it down, so that I could learn to use this myself—"Ladies and Gentlemen, if you're tired, give me a big smile!" They did, and many even laughed. "If you haven't signed in at the table in the hall yet, would you please do us a big favor? We've got to get your names down, because we have such a world-class staff this summer, and such an unbelievably good session for you today, that you and I are going to change the world. And years from now,

historians are going to want to know exactly who was here...."
There were more smiles and laughter and people began moving
into the hall to sign up.

All of us need to stop every once in a while to do what I call a
"tone check." We need to listen to and look at ourselves and make
sure that the abundant warmth and caring that we have on the
inside is showing on the outside, too.

Tone checks are also important for written materials and signs.
For example, forms that staff are supposed to fill out sometimes
say, "No initials!" instead of "Please print your full name. Thanks!"
A sign on a door in the office may say, "No staff allowed!" when it
could say, "Office staff only, please! Thank you!"

## Think Like a Director and Picture the Parents

Many readers of this book will be camp directors. If you're not,
please *think* like one. If you were in charge of the entire camp,
how would you like *your* administrative staff to act? When supervisors are not sure what to do, thinking like the director can make
it much easier to make good judgments.

In moments of indecision, I've also been guided soundly when
I've made myself imagine that a committee of parents is hovering
above me, watching carefully. And I've also found it useful to ask
myself, "If my own children were in this group, what would I
want to be happening right now? What would I want the staff to
be doing? What would I want the supervisor to be doing?" You'll
find that in most cases, by adding this perspective, these questions
become pretty easy to answer.

## Energy & Expertise by Example

Don't let the fact that you're an administrator make you shelve
your talents for working with children. The best way for staff to
learn how to work effectively with children is for them to watch
people who are good at it and follow their example. When
counselors see supervisors bend their knees or sit on the ground
when listening to children, counselors learn to do this more often.
When we see a group of campers moving in lackluster fashion
between activities and we energetically swoop in with a game of
tag that takes them in the direction of the next thing on their

schedule, that group's counselor and other staff who are passing by learn by observation. When specialists see supervisors walk up to groups and ask lots of questions, accompanied by follow-up questions, the specialists start using more questions in their own teaching.

Supervisors can set the pace for staff. When we are energetic and fun, we set an example that can lead our team to success.

## Chapter Twenty-Three

# Super Tips for SuperVision Success

The following techniques explain how to positively affect the *vision* that staff have of us during our supervision—what people see when they are looking at us. We'll conclude with my favorite and most powerful tip about what we can do when *we* are looking at them.

1. **Be aware of your face.** Sometimes I scrunch my face up when I'm concentrating, and staff who look over in my direction may misunderstand my expression to be one of disappointment, disapproval, or constipation. It may even be that I'm thinking about something totally unrelated to them, but they, of course, won't know that. It's easy for a staff person to mistake a supervisor's squinting in the sun for an indication of concern about the staff person. I've learned to be much more aware of how my facial expressions appear to others when I'm walking the Paths.

2. **Try to keep your hands empty when you walk around camp.** Avoid carrying clipboards, notebooks, flame-throwers, and other objects in your hands. Use a fanny

pack. If you need to bring schedules with you, try to reduce them with a photocopier or a computer scanner so they'll fit in the pack. You will find that when your hands are free, children and staff are more likely to interact with you and invite you to play, which is very important.

3. **Do take notes as you walk around, but write discreetly.** If you want to write something down while visiting crafts, wait to write it until you leave that area. I learned this lesson years ago when I was standing in an athletic field and thought of an idea for a special event. I took the small pad out of my back pocket and jotted the idea down. When I looked up, I saw some staff looking over at me. I realized that they might conclude that I was writing about them. So I learned to be more careful about notetaking. Here are two more suggestions about notes:

   ☐ Organize your notetaking in advance. In the past, I've used differently colored 3 by 5 inch file cards that I can keep in my pocket. Notes for Path 1 go on the white card, Path 2 on the yellow card, and so on. A few additional cards organize messages that I need to give to others, miscellaneous ideas, or other matters. Currently, in place of the cards, I use a very inexpensive and highly durable vinyl notebook. It is a little smaller than my hand, has six rings, and is very flexible, so it fits easily into a pocket or fanny pack. Notes for Paths and other subjects can go into separately tabbed sections.

   ☐ Review your notes at the end of the day to make sure you can read what they say. Clarify the writing if necessary while you can still remember what you were writing about. When I don't do this and I look several days later at a scribbled note that says "down the toilet," I don't always remember whether this was a maintenance item or a comment on the effectiveness of my plan to help a counselor with leadership skills.

4. **When talking with a staff person about his or her group, stand facing the group, not with your back to it.** You'll often be able to observe useful things while doing this.

## My Favorite Supervisor Tip

And now, drum roll please. I've saved my all-time favorite supervisor tip for last:

5. **When observing a group, pick one camper at random and watch her or him, and nothing else, for 90 seconds.** This takes some discipline, because there will probably be many other things that will attract your attention during this time. I find it useful to pretend that I'm a television camera operator covering an event and that my television director has told me to keep the lens only on this one child. You'll be fascinated, I think, with the things that you will see and learn when you try this technique.

   For example, you're watching a girl at volleyball. Nothing else. Ninety seconds. She's jumping in place, waiting for the ball to come to her. She shouts "Here!" several times. No one hits the ball to her. No one answers her. No one looks at her. She stands still for a few moments, unmotivated. Then she gets another burst of energy and shouts at her teammates again, but nobody passes to her or otherwise responds. Now a ball hits the ground near her. She bends down to pick it up, and just as she is closing her hands around it, another girl takes it from her and tosses it to the server. The girl we are watching says "Hey!" No one responds. She stands still again, watching the others. Now she looks away from the court and plays with her hair. Time's up.

   For those ninety seconds, *this was camp for this one girl.* We have to be careful about generalizing—we may have randomly observed an atypical moment. But our Path 5 strifeguard alert light will be on and we may decide to walk over to this group and try an experiment using three simultaneous volleyballs to boost the level of participation for

165

all of the campers while encouraging more interaction. And for sure we will keep an eye on this young lady at other times of the day, as well as speak to the counselor, to check what kinds of connections she is making and determine if she needs any extra support.

## Chapter Twenty-Four

# We Will Path
# This Way Again...

Every time we walk on an actual path at camp, we can notice something new and different that we may not have noticed before. I hope the same will be true for you as you walk the Paths of the SuperVision system described in this book.

The Paths are not a final destination. They are a process. They give us direction. We walk the Paths hoping to learn more each time and to keep reaching for greater success. This helps keep our job challenging and interesting throughout the camp season, year after year.

Thank you for reading this book. And most importantly, thank you for dedicating yourself to helping our children find their own paths to fulfilling, wonderful lives.

# The Liver

# Liver A

# SOSS: Xcellent Xamples

As you review the following examples of SOSS (signs of super staff, described in Chapter Seven), please remember that the categories under which they are listed are intended only for general organizational purposes. Many skills could easily fit under more than one category.

Also, it's easy to feel overwhelmed sometimes when we realize that we could spend a lifetime mastering such long lists of skills. Frankly, I like the fact that we are working in a challenging field where there are so many things to learn and refine. Think how boring it would be to have one of those jobs (and there are many) where it takes only a few skills to get the work done. So please view these lists as opportunities for continued growth.

## GROUP LEADERSHIP

### What does X do and say to make X such a superb group leader?

1.  learns the campers' names as quickly as possible and uses their names

2.  knows and can state where every camper is all of the time (if this is one of her or his responsibilities); regularly

counts or otherwise scans the group to make sure every camper is accounted for

3. pays particular attention to which campers she or he sits with or walks with, and varies this to build relationships with all campers

4. pays extra attention to campers who require it; monitors how this time is spent to ensure that it does not result in ignoring or depriving other campers in the group (notifies supervisors when this becomes a problem—please see Teamwork & Responsibility section)

5. smiles

6. speaks in a pleasant voice to campers, even when telling them what to do; pleasant means reasonable volume, respectful, kind, a warm tone, and a manner that would be used when speaking with friends

7. gives campers responsibilities in the group every day, and is creative in finding these; the tasks go beyond "carrying the counselor's clipboard" to more meaningful ones such as leading the discussion about what will be done by the group in free time

8. sits with campers at large group events like morning flagpole gatherings, campfires, and special events

9. makes transition time between activities interesting and fun (leads cheers, does songs, plays tag or other games, plays follow the leader, has group "sneak up" on another staff person)

10. uses "unscheduled time" (waiting to enter building for meals, etc.) to lead games, have conversation, and otherwise engage campers

11. speaks enthusiastically during games and other activities to motivate campers

12. provides commentary with instructional content to campers during activities (not just "keep it going!" but "eye on the ball" and "look around; see who's open....")

13. is in the center of the "action" when leading activities

14. actively and enthusiastically participates in activities with campers and uses her or his own participation to maximize camper involvement (for example, keeps a ball in bounds or passes to people who aren't being passed to)

15. makes positive statements about what she or he likes, to model positive attitudes ("this is my favorite....")

16. in an activity area that is not one of her or his favorites, keeps these beliefs private and presents positive attitudes to campers, or at least models how we can participate in something even if it is not our favorite

17. adds "How can we do this differently?" and "What can I do in this activity that will be unexpected or otherwise take campers by surprise?" to add creativity to program leadership

18. is prepared with alternate plans or additional impromptu activities; thinks ahead by bringing extra materials or equipment in case they are needed

19. puts ordinary adult "coolness" aside and acts silly, goofy, and fun (talks into a banana)

20. goes first to get campers to follow (instead of pointing at the ground to get campers to sit, sits first and beckons for campers to join her or him; when wanting campers to line up, stands in the place where the line should begin and says "Everyone line up behind me, please")

21. uses appropriate touching for effective leadership, especially handshakes; also high-fives, touches on shoulders, and other types of touching that are within camp guidelines

22. helps campers develop special or "secret" positive group behaviors such as handshakes, passwords, and rituals, to build a unique group identity

23. makes keeping the group together a game to prevent wandering (for example, when she or he shouts or says a certain code word of the day, campers run to her or him immediately; they practice this to make it one of the group's basic skills)

24.  leads activities in which campers must work frequently with different partners to encourage the building of teamwork and friendships

25.  runs and moves energetically at times (this doesn't have to be constant) to model and generate energy in the group

26.  whenever possible, allows campers freedom without unnecessary restrictions (for example, straight lines or waiting with backs against a wall are often not really required for management of the group)

27.  frequently gives campers choices about what they will do and how they will do it, to build responsibility and teamwork

28.  when appropriate, uses problems or challenges that arise as positive opportunities to have the group define problems, brainstorm options, and decide what to do; frequently says to campers, "OK, so how do we solve/handle this?"

29.  has regular "meetings" with the group to talk about how things are going, what campers like and what they don't, and to provide a regular outlet for expressing feelings

30.  learns about and can state each camper's most important needs, interests, and goals and makes efforts to help tailor activities in response to these

## TEACHING

### What does X do and say to make X such a superb teacher?

1.  before teaching an activity or lesson, prepares and can state what specific skill goal or goals she or he will be working on with campers (e.g. shot placement in tennis, base-running strategy in baseball, color mixing in art, give-and-take in drama, ball-stopping control in soccer) and why they are important

2.  clearly communicates these specific goals at the beginning of activities or lessons

3.  before teaching an activity or lesson, decides and can state how to determine at its conclusion whether campers

learned the specific goal or goals

4.  before teaching an activity or lesson, decides and communicates specific and meaningful jobs and responsibilities to assisting staff or to counselors who are bringing their group to the area ("Chris, I'd appreciate it if you would do two things during this period. We're going to be working today just on lower body stuff, especially knees and how the feet move. So after I explain this and we start to practice, I'd like it if you would walk around and double check them to be sure they are keeping their knees bent, not locked. Then we'll do a little practice relay to help with the feet, and I'll show the whole group how it works. Then we'll split into two groups so they get more turns; you'll lead one group, in a way I'll show you, and I'll lead the other group....")

5.  breaks skills into smaller skills or steps so that they can be learned more easily

6.  praises campers for accomplishing intermediate steps, not just for completion of the entire task, so that positive feedback is provided throughout the process and not only at the end

7.  as steps are accomplished, has campers stop and show what they've done so far so that the staff person can make sure everyone is on track, and so that campers can celebrate success and build confidence as they continue to learn

8.  numbers steps to be accomplished and uses the numbers to keep the presentation organized ("There are three steps to getting this right; let's start with step one....")

9.  repeatedly and cumulatively reviews what's been learned before moving on to further steps ("OK, so the important thing about step one is to do ABC; now let's try step two....")

10.  helps campers learn by guiding them to the "big picture" through repeated references to the few key points that she or he believes are most important; asks the question, "If my campers learned nothing else in this activity or lesson,

the one specific thing that would be most important would be..."

11. shows and demonstrates things whenever possible instead of just explaining them in words

12. has campers come up in front to assist in demonstrations for greater clarity and attention (for example, instead of demonstrating a backhand in tennis, the instructor has a camper stand next to her or him and the instructor shows that camper how to do it properly; now both of them demonstrate it)

13. has assistants or group counselors come up front to assist in demonstrations, to directly involve them

14. varies the volume of her or his voice

15. varies the speed of her or his voice

16. "underlines" important words by varying volume and using gestures and facial expressions, for both attention and clarity

17. uses pauses to emphasize particularly important teaching points

18. varies where she or he stands, and moves from time to time to get and maintain attention

19. uses substantially more questions than statements (asks, "So if we want this baseball swing to be faster, where do we want the bat to be in relation to the shoulder?" instead of saying, "For a faster swing, we want the bat to be off the shoulder.")

20. asks substantially more open questions than any other type ("Why do we do this?" instead of "Do we do this in order to ABC?")

21. encourages campers to make predictions to build thinking skills ("If we do it this way, what do you think will happen? What would work better?")

22. uses multiple choice formats for reviewing skills ("Should I have my feet here, here, or here? OK, good. Why?")

23. gives lots of opportunities for campers to be directly involved with hands-on activities and practice to maximize camper participation

24. breaks the group into sub-groups and uses assisting staff and group counselors to maximize the number of turns that campers get to practice (for example, has three or four small lines or groups of campers instead of one big one)

25. frequently tries different, novel, creative ways of presenting information and experiences, to take campers by surprise and do the unexpected ("Here's the trick to getting this right. It may be the most important thing we learn this session. And it's sealed in this envelope. Cary, would you open it for us? OK, inside is another envelope. T.J., would you open that one? And Pat, would you read the paper that's inside?...")

26. precisely plans the first minute or two of an activity or lesson to grab attention

27. begins with an attention-grabbing statement—"Well, I suppose I should tell you now because you're going to find out anyway...."

28. begins with an interesting question or problem or challenge that campers can answer or resolve by participating in the activity or lesson—"OK, good morning, everybody. Here's the situation. You and your partner are in one boat (gets campers to stand up behind her or him) heading this way when another boat comes out of nowhere right in your path, like this (gets two more campers up and into position). Three questions, and we've got to ask and answer them fast because we've only got about 2 seconds to decide. Question one, how much insurance do we have? Question two, which way do I turn? Question three, what's the fastest and best way for me to make the turn? Today we're going to experiment, figure out what works best, and practice getting it done...."

29. to review past learning, build confidence in campers, and motivate further learning, begins activities and lessons with a quick opportunity for campers to demonstrate their

knowledge or competence about something that everyone in the group has already solidly mastered ("Before we keep working on getting our horses to turn, everybody please show us how we hold the reins; excellent!")

30. plans and leads activities or lessons so there are different phases or parts done at varied paces and with varied types of participation (in a field sport, for example, the first ten minutes are spent on several fast, fun relays that reinforce important skills; the next 10 minutes include a demonstration of two advanced skills with opportunities to practice first individually and then with a partner; two-thirds into the session a game is played, during which is a 7-minute "power period" of fun and creative rule variations; followed by more regular play; concluding with a quick 2-minute skill challenge)

31. "feeds" campers eyes by holding up objects to get and maintain attention; also has people up front for the same purpose

32. provides clear instructions by showing not only what to do but what *not* to do, using a positive tone ("Everybody look up here, please. See the way I'm holding this? I've got it cramped up next to my body. That's going to mess it up. Here's the better way. I'm going to hold it out in front of me, relaxed, like this. Now what makes that better?....")

33. in demonstrations, sometimes turns and faces the same way campers are facing so that campers see things from their perspective

34. makes references to right and left handedness to take into account differences between campers ("If you're a lefty, you'll do it like this....")

35. makes frequent use of repetition because saying the same thing in a few different ways is an effective way to enhance learning

36. increases attention and motivates learning by explaining when, where, and how she or he learned the skill

37. increases attention and motivates learning by, when appropriate, making what is taught special or unique ("The part we're going to work on today isn't known to most people. You can find people out there who have been doing this for two or three years and they still don't know this....")

38. models respect by always saying "please" when telling people what to do

39. demonstrates patience by saying "Take your time...."

40. helps campers deal with the stress of learning by telling them in advance, if true, that when she or he, their instructor, first learned how to do this, it didn't come out perfectly the first or first few times, and then explaining how she or he learned to do it better

41. when a particular step does not have to be done perfectly, tells this to campers

42. anticipates questions by incorporating expected ones into the instruction ("Now there's two things that a lot of people wonder about when they're trying this....")

43. waits to hand out stuff to campers during initial explanations so that they will listen better and not be distracted by playing with what has just been passed out

44. provides time for campers' questions and treats them as important by fully answering them and also encouraging others to participate in responding to the question

45. praises campers when they ask questions ("I'm so glad you asked that. That's how smart people learn, by asking questions..."—"That question really helps us, because....")

46. praises campers for admitting out loud that they don't know what to do or that they don't understand, which in turn creates an atmosphere in which others who may be more reluctant to admit this feel that they are safe to do the same thing

47. praises campers for expressing curiosity, treasuring questions such as "How does this work?" and "Why does this happen?" and "What's inside of this?" and "Who

thought this up – where did it come from?" and "Why do people do that?" and statements like "I wonder...."; she or he models the importance of such questions or statements by using them

48. praises campers who display more in-depth thinking by giving reasons for things or examples

49. creates a positive environment for learning by praising campers who help others or show others how to do things

50. helps campers measure their individual progress by commenting on specific things they can do better or have improved

51. praises campers for showing signs of critical thinking, like when they say, "What if....?" and "Is it possible....?" and "What would happen if....?" and "Is there another way?"

52. praises campers for noticing details ("Most people don't notice that" and "It would take most people a long time before they saw that; that was very observant...")

53. praises campers for persistence and concentration ("You've been working on this a long time" and "You keep trying this until you get it; that's really hard work")

54. gives campers frequent opportunities to learn from each other, applying the important teaching maxim, "We've never really learned something until we've had to teach it to another." (e.g. by having each camper turn to a learning partner, after a step or series of steps, and check each other out to be sure they are each doing OK)

55. provides opportunities for camper input by asking campers what they want to learn and giving them choices about how they want to learn it, what they want to do first, and so on

56. asks campers and other staff "What do you think?" and gets their opinions about the activities or lessons

57. not only asks for input, but immediately changes the way activities or lessons are presented based on her or his own evaluation and the input of campers and other staff who have participated earlier

58. has alternative activities or teaching tools prepared and uses them to flexibly respond to campers' responses and needs

59. supportively calls on campers to answer questions even if they don't volunteer, guiding them to good responses by rephrasing questions or making them easier

60. for campers who do not participate in discussion or do not volunteer to answer questions, asks questions "on their behalf" to increase attention and participation; this is done by saying, "Now, you know, Greg (a camper who has not been participating) is standing here and looking at this and he's wondering, 'What's the big deal about doing it this way? Why can't you just hold it any way you want?' Which is a very smart question. Would somebody please talk about that for a minute...?" (it may not be Greg who responds; the instructor has anyone respond, but Greg is now wide awake and paying close attention)

61. uses campers' names when posing hypothetical situations, which personalizes instruction and increases attention ("Suppose Roxanne were to come around one of us on the side like this; what would we do?")

62. attempts to individualize instruction to whatever extent possible by assessing each camper's needs and giving them opportunities during a learning period to work on skills that are appropriate for their level of competency; for example, includes time in activities and lessons for such individual practice and uses assistants and group counselors to work with individuals on specific skills

63. accommodates the wide variety of campers' learning styles by using a variety of teaching techniques whenever possible; for example, teaching a skill by talking about it, having campers talk about it, using lots of visuals and hands-on experiences, having campers work and practice in groups as well as by themselves, and so on

64. when leading discussion, encourages campers to speak to each other and not just to the instructor (says, "tell them")

65. previews directions by providing campers an opportunity to picture what they will do and then having them actually do it (says, "In a moment, not yet, what we're going to do is....")

66. presents rules or policies in a positive and more interactive way by first asking campers, "What are good choices to make?" in the activity or lesson area and then asking them to identify bad choices; asks campers to explain why these are good or bad to facilitate understanding of opportunities, expectations, and rules

67. corrects campers by making positive suggestions to do things better ("If you try holding it this way, it should be easier to grab" instead of "No, that's not the way I showed you how to do this....")

68. praises campers for making positive changes and helps them notice the improvement by saying things like, "You found a better way to do this...."

69. designs activities and lessons to encourage campers to learn through self-discovery and experience instead of lecture

70. frequently uses sophisticated vocabulary, even with younger campers, casually defining words right after using them so that children learn better ways of expressing themselves ("This is symmetrical, it's the same on both sides, and that helps with balance because...")

71. increases group participation and learning by having campers "fill in blanks" as she or he speaks ("We're telling the horse how to move, not just with our hands but with our—(pause; if needed, shakes legs as a clue)—legs, yes; and when we're turning to the left, we press with our leg on the—which side is it?")

72. increases active involvement and learning by frequently getting the entire group to answer questions out loud at the same time, like a chorus

73. has campers speak steps out loud to help them retain information ("Step, throw, and follow through; step, throw, and follow through....")

74. develops deeper learning and good thinking skills in campers by having them make comparisons between things and talk about the differences ("What's the difference between this and this?")

## COMMUNICATION

### What does X do and say to be such an excellent communicator?

1. makes one-on-one eye contact with campers, even when greeting a group of them (i.e. takes a second to individually notice each one)

2. when listening, especially to important feelings, bends knees or sits or leans to demonstrate that she or he is staying and focusing on what is being said

3. encourages campers to communicate feelings by frequently saying things like, "Tell me about that" and "I want to hear about that" and just "Tell me...."

4. praises campers for communication by saying things like, "I'm glad you're telling me this" and "Thanks for telling me this out loud" and "You're doing a good job letting me know how you feel..." and "It's good that you can talk about this, because it's important for me to know what you're thinking...."

5. when campers speak about feelings, holds back his or her own responses to provide "multiple turns" to campers so that they can have more practice putting their feelings into words

6. takes advantage of meal times, "down time" and time between scheduled activities to engage campers in conversation, one-on-one and in groups

7. makes others feel that they really have been heard by stating what she or he "got" from what was said; uses this skill especially when listening to upset feelings; says,

"You're mad because...." and then summarizes what the camper has said

8. when people are upset, asks them, "Do you believe that I get what you're saying/feeling here?"

9. demonstrates awareness of the content of communication by making sure that many conversations are about subjects that the campers care about and not just about behavior management or program matters

10. asks campers follow-up questions to encourage more communication

11. is quiet when others are speaking and waits for them to finish

## TEAMWORK & RESPONSIBILITY

**What does X do and say to be so excellent working with co-staff and administrators?**

1. shows appreciation for the work of other team members, and models this for campers, by having her or his group thank specialists and instructors at the conclusion of an activity or lesson

2. shows appreciation for the work of other team members by taking campers into the kitchen, maintenance areas, and other places where people labor somewhat invisibly and introducing campers to these people, letting them see "backstage" where the work is done

3. tells supervisor if she or he needs help; does this as soon as this is realized

4. when asking for help, defines the problem, tells what she or he has done or tried so far, and then asks for additional ideas

5. tells supervisors if campers need help; informs supervisor promptly when campers are frequently sitting out of activities or having other important problems

6. offers help to others even when not directly obligated or expected to do so, saying things like, "How can I help?"

and "What do you need?" and "Is there anything else I can do?"

7. demonstrates initiative by doing helpful things without or before being asked

8. does more than is expected to do or more than is included in her or his specific job description (day camp counselor calls parents as soon as she or he arrives at camp to let them know that their daughter stopped crying a block from their house)

9. picks up litter, equipment, and other things even if she or he did not cause the mess

10. displays a positive attitude by saying things like, "We can do this" and talking about the benefits and positive sides of things

11. thanks people when they make suggestions

12. demonstrates listening to the suggestions of others by using follow-up questions to get more detail ("Well, OK, when you say that I have to look like I'm not taking sides between Cory and Jo, what are some good ways to show them that?"

13. asks people for suggestions on how to improve ("Do you have any ideas of how I could do ABC?")

14. initiates greetings: says hello first when approaching others (it's fun, by the way, when everyone at camp tries to do this!)

15. asks others how they are doing; demonstrates that this is not perfunctory courtesy by following up later with questions about what others said ("Hey, Jill, how is that skit coming that you were worried about yesterday?")

16. at meetings of staff, is quiet while others are speaking

17. when working with other staff, frequently asks them for their ideas about how things should be done ("What do you think?")

18. changes her or his mind when it appears that someone else's view or another idea is better

19.  encourages others to state their views, even if different, by saying things like, "Who's got the other side of this?" and "What are some other ways we could do this or think about this?" and "What haven't we thought of?"

20.  demonstrates "give and take" and flexibility by compromising and sometimes letting others do things the way they think is best

21.  supports team decisions even if they are different from her or his personal views, but if her or his personal views are different on important issues, speaks up respectfully to put these views "on the table" instead of keeping it inside or saying it behind people's backs; "respectfully" means speaking about the issue and not personalities, prefacing comments by using language such as, "I hope that it's OK to say what I think about this, because it is different, and I would like you to consider it...."

22.  if staff put others down or talk behind others' backs, asks people not to do this; if she or he thinks of such comments herself or himself, demonstrates discipline by keeping these unspoken

23.  keeps promises; does what she or he says will be done

24.  keeps on the schedule; if wants to vary from the schedule, speaks to a supervisor before doing so

25.  shows up on time and sometimes even earlier than necessary, just to be ready

26.  brings whatever materials or equipment are expected

27.  follows rules and meets expectations even when administrators are not present, demonstrating belief in the maxim, "integrity is what we do when no one is looking"

28.  shows awareness of the behavior of campers and groups for which she or he is not directly responsible by tactfully and respectfully speaking to them if they are breaking rules or not acting the way they are supposed to; tactfully and respectfully means showing sensitivity for other staff persons' authority when doing so, by bringing campers to their leader; when this is done repeatedly and the other

leader does not seem to be handling these situations responsibly, then she or he confers with a supervisor by saying things like, "I don't mean to put my nose in this, but I would like your advice in handling this...." or "I'd like to know what you think is the best thing for me to do when...."

29. admits fault by saying things like, "This was my mistake" and "I did it"

30. handles mistakes by focusing on what should be done better next time, saying things like, "Next time I will do ABC" and can state why that would be a better choice

31. shares credit with others and gives credit by saying things like *"our* event" and *"our* idea" and "It was Cheryl's suggestion"

32. gives other people opportunities to lead by asking them to step into a role that she or he could have performed; if she or he has had an earlier opportunity to do something, remains quiet and lets others volunteer

## BEHAVIOR MANAGEMENT

### What does X do and say that makes X so excellent in handling behavior in positive ways?

1. anticipates problems and "heads them off at the pass" by speaking with campers in advance and helping campers to think about how to behave; for example, before a hike, briefly discusses with them (as opposed to lectures about) good and bad choices to make during a hike

2. calls meetings to resolve problems in the group, giving the campers responsibility to work out solutions together

3. teaches campers how to resolve conflicts by giving each involved person an opportunity to state the problem and how they feel, getting them to listen to each other by stating the views of the other people involved, and having them figure out what they want and how to compromise if necessary

4. when speaking to campers who have made bad choices, demonstrates calmness and confidence by using a normal volume and speaking slowly

5. when speaking to campers who have made bad choices, makes eye contact to demonstrate seriousness

6. when speaking to campers who have made bad choices, crouches or sits down to indicate that this is an important moment

7. moves toward those campers who are behaving improperly to demonstrate seriousness; the body language says, "This is important and we need to solve this right now..." and not, "I am trying to intimidate you."

8. uses words to describe how she or he feels when campers do not behave properly, saying things like "I'm really upset that you did that, because you said that you weren't going to do this anymore" and "I'm really disappointed..." and "This makes me feel really angry/frustrated..."

9. after telling campers that what they are doing is not OK, immediately tells campers what they are supposed to do or say to act better ("You can't go in there without asking, it's not allowed; if you want something in there, you just come to me or another staff person and we'll help you get what you need...." or "You can't throw that football in here; if you want to throw it, that's cool, but you have to go outside and throw it so that we make sure nothing gets broken")

10. explains the reasons for rules or expectations to help campers understand how to behave better ("Here is why this is important....")

11. frequently notices and praises positive behavior, stating specifically what was done ("You did that without my having to ask you....")

12. physically demonstrates enthusiasm about positive behavior by looking impressed, doing high-fives, shaking hands, vigorous nodding, and warm, appreciative smiles

# Reverse Engineering: Sample Skill List

We described the reverse engineering process in Chapter Twelve. We ask two questions:

☐ **Question One:** "What do we want people to say about us?"

☐ **Question Two:** "What do people who have those qualities do or say?"

Here are some items that you can add to the lists that I hope you made on your own. Please note that numbered items will often fit under more than one heading. For example, items under "Cares About the Ideas of Others" would probably also be examples of "Teamwork."

## Careful, Meticulous, Thorough

1. "Is there anything that we haven't considered?" and "What have we left out?"

2. "Is there anyone that we haven't spoken to about this that we should speak to?"

3. "What could go wrong?"

4.  before implementing a plan, considers alternate or back-up plans: "What will we do if X goes wrong, Y doesn't happen, or Z does happen?"

5.  double checks things: "Let's go over this again." and "Is this right?"

## Considerate

1.  "I'm worried about Amy . . . ."

2.  "What will Lee think if we do that?"

3.  "Are you OK?" and "How are you feeling?"

4.  speaks to people privately to avoid risk of embarrassing them

5.  follows up by asking about someone or something that had been commented on earlier: "How is _____ doing/going?"

6.  stands up for or defends others: "Don't say that about him..." and "Leave her alone..." and "Get off his case...."

7.  reacts unfavorably in response to gossip, put-downs, hurtful comments, or jokes at others' expense; chooses not to repeat gossip

8.  even when busy, tries to help another person

9.  sends supportive notes or messages, particularly when there is no social obligation to do so

## Creative

1.  "Is there another way we could do this?"
    "What's every way this could be done?"
    "How can it be done differently?"

2.  "Why?" and "How come?" and "Why not?"

3.  "What if?" and "What about this...?"

4.  "What else?" and "You know what else we could do..."

5.  "How does that work?"

6.  "Why are we doing this?" and "Why does it have to be done this way?"

7.  "Let's think some more about this"
    "Let's look at this another way..."

8.  "Or..." and "And..." and "Also..."

9.  does things differently than before

10. tests and experiments: "Let's try and see..." and "Could we..." and "Suppose..."

11. develops appropriate, efficient short-cuts: "How do we get around this?"

## Enthusiastic

1.  "This is my favorite." and "This is the best."

2.  "Let's do this again."

3.  "Wait 'til you hear this!" and "You've got to hear/see this!"

4.  "This is a great idea!"

5.  smiles

6.  arrives early

7.  leaves meetings still talking about the subjects

8.  does extra

9.  talks fast and uses higher volume sometimes to express excitement or conviction

10. stands up or moves around to explain something

11. moves briskly when getting things, passing things out, etc.

## Flexible and Open-Minded

1.  "I'm changing my mind."

2.  "I thought this, but now I think this..."

3.  "I used to do it this way; now I do it this better way...."

4.  "I'll hold up judgment here until we know more..." and "I'll wait and see..."

5.  "OK, I'll do that if you do this."

6.  "What's the other side of this?"

7.  tries new ideas, methods: "I don't agree, but let's try it and see." and "I'll go along with it…"

8.  listens to more than one point of view

## Forgiving

1.  "That's OK." and "I forgive you."

2.  "These things happen."

3.  "Not your fault, don't worry."

4.  "Try again."

5.  "It's over, forget it."

6.  "Nobody's perfect."

7.  "We've all done it."

8.  "It's not so bad. We can fix it."

9.  "Couldn't be helped."

10. "Let's start over."

11. re-initiates positive contact after a negative incident

## Hard Worker & Industrious

1.  acts beyond the call of duty; does more than is required

2.  to get something done, stays late, comes in early, or shows up when not required to do so

3.  volunteers: "I'll do it."

4.  does things *before* she or he is asked to do them

5.  does things over again if not done correctly the first time

## Honest & Open

1.  "I'm not comfortable with that…"

2.  "I'm worried / afraid / scared / concerned."

3.  "I don't like that."

4.  "It hurts my feelings when you do/say that."

5.  "It was really Pat's idea/work."

6.  "I never thought of that." and "I didn't know."

7.  "I don't know how to do this." and "I need help." and "I

don't understand; would you explain it again?" and "Show me how to do this, please."

8.  "I'm not so good at this; this isn't my strength."

9.  says things that are hard but important to say

10. says something useful that she or he is not obligated to say

11. expresses an opinion or view that is different from those held by others

## Humor

1.  laughs at non-hurtful stuff

2.  smiles or laughs at herself or himself to show she or he is not perfect

3.  takes a bow or says "good one" when making a small mistake or misstatement

4.  smiles when doing hard things and says "This is hard."

## Listener

1.  "Tell me more..."

2.  makes eye contact

3.  reacts with facial expressions to show attentiveness

4.  takes notes

5.  repeats or rephrases what is being said from time to time "I want to be sure that I've got this...."

6.  asks questions to clarify what has been said "Is this what you're saying?"

7.  is silent while others are speaking—doesn't talk or interrupt when they are talking

8.  balances the amount of time spent talking and listening

9.  adds to what the person is saying

## Organized

1.  "How should we get this done?"

2.  "What needs to be done to make this happen?" "What are the steps?"

3. "What/who is needed to accomplish this?"

4. "In what order do we have to do these things?" "What's the next thing to do?"

5. "Who wants to do what?" "Who would be best at doing this step/part?"

6. delegates

7. numbers points or steps: "There are three reasons..." "Number one..." and "First..."

8. makes lists; prioritizes list items

9. does first what's most important: "The most important..."

10. puts things back where they were found

11. has specific labels on things; labels things clearly so that they can be used by others

12. finds things quickly because they are accessible

13. has lots of folders instead of one big one with everything in it

14. takes time to manage time: makes a plan as to how time will be used: "How much time is worth spending on this?"

## Patient

1. "I'll wait."

2. "Take your time." and "Don't rush..."

3. "You let me know when you're ready."

4. waits for others to speak first

5. waits for people to finish speaking

## Positive, Persistent, & Optimistic

1. speaks about positive benefits or advantages

2. "I'll try." and "Let's try it."

3. "Let's try again." and "Let's do it over." and "We can get it right."

4. "I/we can do this."

5. compliments others; compliments self

6. accepts compliments of others: "Thank you, I appreciate your saying that." and "It's important to me that you liked it."

## Problem Solver

1. "What is the problem here?" and "What do you think the problem is?"
2. "What is your view?"
3. "I want to state what your side is to be sure that I understand it; would you do the same so that we can both be sure that we've heard each other?"
4. "Do you believe that I understand what you're saying?"
5. "What are our options?" and "What's every possible way we could solve this?"
6. "Is the option we're trying now working?"
7. "What else can we do or try that might work better?"
8. presents problems with possible solutions
9. demonstrates positive attitude about problems: "That's what we do here, handle problems."

## Respectful & Polite

1. "Please..."
2. "Thank you."
3. "Excuse me."
4. "Sir" and "Ma'am" and "Ladies and gentlemen"
5. learns and uses people's names
6. introduces herself or himself to others
7. holds doors open; helps carry things
8. gets out of people's way (before asked)
9. picks up things that others dropped
10. does things the first time asked

## Responsible

1. "I was wrong." and "I did it." and "I messed up."

2.  "You're right."

3.  "I'm sorry."

4.  "I should have done it this way."

5.  "Please forgive me."

6.  "What can I do to make up for this?"

7.  accepts criticism or comments from others by asking follow-up questions, inviting more, reporting changes made as a result of the communication

8.  arrives on time

9.  completes tasks when due

10. delivers what has been promised

11. says when she or he can't do something or be someplace, with adequate notice to get it covered or handled in another way

## Team Player

1.  "How can I help you?" and "What can I do for you?"

2.  "What do you need?"

3.  "Here, use mine." and "Would you like some?"

4.  "You go first."

5.  "I'll trade you."

6.  "I'll cover for you."

7.  "I couldn't have done this without you."

8.  "I'm going to X; can I get you anything while I'm there?"

9.  "Join us." "Come with me."

10. "Let's work on this together."

11. shows people how to do things

12. interprets for someone: "He means XYZ..."

13. warns of pitfalls ahead

14. gives important or useful information: "Did you know...?"

15. provides constructive criticism or coaching: "Try it this way..."

16. makes eye contact and says hello or good morning or otherwise initiates conversation with everyone, not just the "regulars" that she or he is closest to

17. "What are you working on?" and "I'm working on this..."

18. focuses on expertise of others: "Sue can do this, she's good at this..."

19. says "we" and "our"

## Values the Views of Others

1. "What do you think?" and "Can I bounce this off of you...?" and "How do you feel about this?" and "How does this sound / look?"

2. "Bev, you haven't spoken about this; how do you feel...?"

3. "Tell me why you feel that way..."

4. "Have you ever been in a situation where . . . .?

5. "What do you think I / we should do?"

6. "How do you want to do it?"

7. "Is it OK if we do it this way?"

8. "I am glad you told me that out loud and didn't keep it to yourself..."

9. "Let her finish..."

10. gets others quiet so someone can speak: "Shhhh!!!"

11. asks how their conduct will affect others: "If I change this, will that mess up what you're working on?"

12. helps keep conversation on track: "OK, so you were saying..." and "Getting back to what Steve said...."

# Questions That Help Teach Problem-Solving to Staff

We described in Chapter Fourteen how to use questions to help build better thinking and decision-making skills in staff. Here are some more questions we can use for this purpose:

## Questions that help define a problem

The first step in solving a problem is figuring out what it is. Sometimes staff know that there is a problem or that something isn't going the way it should, but they have difficulty being specific about what is going on or how they want it to change. For example, they might want campers to be "nicer to each other" but they may not have figured out the positive behaviors that they are looking for. Or the staff person might tell you that a camper is "driving them crazy" but they may not have taken the time to identify the specific behaviors that are causing the problems. These questions are terrific tools to get staff thinking more specifically:

1.  What do you feel about X (the issue or problem or challenge)?

2.  What do you want to change?

3.  Why do you want it changed?

4.  What do you believe would happen if things continued the way they are now?

5.  Why do you believe things would be better if they changed in the way we're talking about?

6.  What do *you* want to have happen?

7.  What's the most important thing that you want to have happen?

8.  What is it that we want people to do differently?

9.  What do you wish people were doing instead?

10. If the situation were the way you wanted it to be, what would it look like—what would you actually see people doing?

11. If the situation were the way you wanted it to be, what would you hear them saying—what would their actual words be?

12. What is it specifically that we want to accomplish—what would you say is the goal here?

13. If we could wave a wand and make things the way we want them to be, what would they look like—how would you describe them?

14. Picture the ideal situation you're looking for: how is it different from what you're seeing now?

15. What troubles you about what is happening now? How would you put it into words?

16. You're saying that they're driving you crazy. What was the last thing that you can remember them doing that made you feel that way?

17. What first made you believe that they were acting so badly—what did they do?

18. Has it always been this bad? If not, then what do you think has made it change?

## Questions that help staff identify potential options

1.  What are our options?

2.  What choices do we have here?

3.  What can be done about this?

4.  Let's brainstorm a minute: what's every possible way we could resolve this?

5.  What do we need to know in order to make a good decision about this? How would we find these things out?

## Questions that help staff consider and evaluate options

1.  How do we decide what to do?

2.  How should we decide which option is best?

3.  Which options should we eliminate?

4.  How do we know if this is a good idea or a bad idea? What can we do to find out?

5.  How can we test this before we try it for real?

6.  What might go wrong?

7.  Are there any down sides to this one?

8.  What are the benefits/advantages to this one?

9.  What do you think about the possible costs versus the possible benefits?

10. What do you believe people will conclude/believe/think if we do X?

11. What do you think will happen if we do X?

12. What is the best case scenario if we do X?

13. What is the worst case scenario if we do X?

14. What do you believe is the likelihood of success or failure of X?

15. What do you think this option would cost—not necessarily in terms of money, but in time, people involved, favors traded in, and other resources?

## Questions that help staff make sure that they've been comprehensive in their thinking

Sometimes when we think through things with staff, we will be aware that there are some things that they haven't thought about but should. Of course we could just tell them what those items are, but the following questions give staff practice in identifying these themselves.

1. Have we left anything out?

2. Have we left anyone out—is there anyone else who should be involved in this, or who we should speak to?

3. What's the other side of this?

4. Are there any *other* ways do this?

5. How could we do this differently?

6. If there were someone here with more experience with this sort of situation, what do you think they would say about it?

7. Do you think anyone else has ever confronted this kind of situation before? How can we find out what they did or what happened? How can we learn from what they did instead of starting from scratch?

8. Do you wish we had more time to think about this? If we did, what would we do?

9. Since we don't have any more time to think about this, what can we do to make sure that this is the best thing to do?

10. If we gave this some more thought, do you think we might come up with something else? Would it be worth it just to make sure that we haven't left anything out?

## Questions that help staff look at things from the perspective of others

1.  If you were in A's position (or, for example, my position) at this point, what would your next move be?

2.  What do you guess A is feeling about this?

3.  How do you think A wants to feel about this?

4.  If A were here right now, what do you think A would be saying?

## Questions that help staff begin solving the problem and evaluate progress

1.  What are the steps we should take at this point?

2.  What should we do (needs to be done) first?

3.  Where do you think is the best place to start?

4.  What is the first thing that you want to have happen?

5.  What do you think is the most important thing to have happen?

6.  If you could only do or try one thing in this situation and not anything else, what would that one thing be?

7.  What's the next step?

8.  What's the best way to get that done (make that happen)?

9.  When do you think is the best time to make that happen?

10. If we try this option/plan, how will we know if it is working the way that we want it to?

11. Do you think we should have a back-up plan in advance? What do you think it should be?

12. So we've got a plan. Let's review: who's going to do what?

13. How will we know if this is working?

14. What should we do if what we've decided to try doesn't seem to be working?

15. When should we talk about this again?

## Questions that help staff set deadlines and get assistance

1. What do you think is a reasonable time in which to get this thing (or this step) accomplished?

2. Have you done this sort of thing before? If not, what should we do about estimating the time that will be needed—should we add or take away?

3. If it is going to take more time than we've guessed, what should you do if you think that we won't meet the deadline? Who should you talk to about that? When should you talk about it?

4. If you have problems or questions as you work on this, how do you want to handle that?

5. What if you feel you may need help but you're worried about what people will think—what do you want to do about that?

## Questions that help staff make the best use of available resources

1. Who could we talk to about this?

2. Who around here knows the most about this sort of thing?

3. Who is the best person to help make this happen?

4. What can I do to be of help to you with this?

5. What would you like me to do? How would you like me to be involved?

6. What other information would be valuable for us to have? How could we get it?

## Questions that help staff handle their own resistance or negativism

1. What's going through your mind when we're talking about this stuff? Is there anything that makes you feel uncomfortable or worried about what's going to happen?

2. Is there someone else that you think you would be more comfortable talking to about this?

3.  (when only negative comments are made) That's the negative side, and it's important to know what that is. Now what's the positive side?

4.  (if they can't or won't say anything positive) What if someone said that ABC is a positive side—what would you think about that?

5.  (if they make global complaints, as in "nothing is right") Which part of this situation/plan/idea is not OK with you? What's the worst part—the one that you think is most important?

6.  If we don't do anything differently about this situation, what do you expect will happen? How do you feel about that?

7.  What if you had to do some work to make this problem go away—would you be willing to do that? Does it depend on how hard you'd have to work? What if you didn't have to do that work yourself—what if someone were willing to do it with you?

8.  Would you be willing to think about this some more before you decide whether there is any way to fix it?

9.  Would you say that this is a very simple problem or kind of a complicated one? If it's more of a complicated one, then would you expect that to be easier or harder to solve?

10. How long do you think it took for this problem to develop? What does that tell you about how much time it might take to make it go away?

11. If we can't make this problem completely go away, would you consider it worth it if we could at least make some of it better?

12. Would you rather that I just told you what to do? Why do you think that is? Why would that be more comfortable?

## What to Do When You Get Tired of All These Questions and Feel an Irrepressible Urge to Lecture

You can always just say what you're thinking and discuss it with the staff person. It's often more effective, though, to try to first present your ideas in the form of another question, to get the staff person to think about it and respond. You can ask it in this way: "What if someone were to say ABC (here we state the idea or view that we believe the staff person has not considered)? What would you say about that?"

## The Big Bonus

Please remember that we can use these questions to guide ourselves when we need to solve problems and make our own decisions.

# About the Author

Michael Brandwein is the author of the number one best-selling books in three areas of the camp industry: training (*Training Terrific Staff*), supervision (*Super Staff SuperVision*), and leadership development (*Learning Leadership: How to Develop Outstanding Teen Leadership Training Programs at Camp*). Michael is one of the top experts on training people to work with children and youth. He has made presentations in all 50 of the U.S. states, in almost every province of Canada, and on 6 of the 7 continents. He is a frequent staff development presenter for camps, recreation programs, schools, businesses, and other professional associations. Michael has presented national keynotes for many organizations, including the American Camp Association, the Canadian Camping Association, and the National Recreation and Park Association. He has received two national honors from the American Camp Association and has served on its national board of directors and executive committee.

Michael wrote and presented three Emmy® award-winning television programs called *Parenting Puzzle: The Middle Years* on communicating with young people which have been broadcast on PBS stations throughout the U.S. Michael's Juris Doctor degree is from the University of Chicago. In past lives, Michael was a trial lawyer and partner for nine years in a 55-member law firm, a writer and performer for two years on a Chicago Emmy® award-winning educational television program, a graduate of Chicago's famed Second City improv theater school, and a professional magician. Michael lives in the Chicago area with his wife Donna, a certified sign language interpreter, and their two children.

Michael Brandwein
5 Coventry Lane / Lincolnshire, IL  60069
Ph: 847-940-9820 / Fax: 847-940-9829
www.michaelbrandwein.com

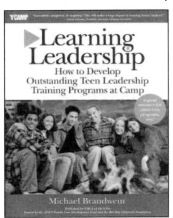